OLD STUFF, NEWER STUFF, AND STUFF

OLD STUFF, NEWER STUFF, AND STUFF

Samuel B Mills
2017

© 2017 Samuel B Mills
All rights reserved.

ISBN-13: 9781546521983
ISBN-10: 1546521984

Connie Harman Mills

Dedicated to my wife Connie Harman Mills, the "EVERYTHING" in my life, and to the Alzheimer's Association which champions an ongoing effort to help those afflicted with Alzheimer's and their caregivers. The fight is not over, but with God's help relief will be on the horizon; both a means of prevention and of curing the dread disease will be found.

Acknowledgement

Thanks to Gloria Roberts Cannon Franklin and Anne Broome Trawick who contributed a superb effort in proofreading this work. English-smart, fun to work with, and with eagle eyes are these long-time friends who helped remove my doo-dahs and produced a polished print copy.

Contents

Acknowledgement · vii
Prologue · xiii

Part I Old Stuff · 1
1   Remembrances of Childhood · · · · · · · · · · · · · · · · · ·3
2   Copperhead Fun· ·8
3   Miss Alma, aka Aunt Alma Adams · · · · · · · · · · · ·12
4   A Changing Landscape· ·15
5   Old Spring Creek Power Dam· · · · · · · · · · · · · · · · ·20
6   What I Miss About Donalsonville · · · · · · · · · · · · ·23
7   The Smokehouse· ·30
8   Solie ·33
9   Fishing· ·35
10 Hoyt and Ozie Butler's Store· · · · · · · · · · · · · · · · · ·38
11 Ugly Picture· ·41
12 The Steyerman House· ·44
13 Hitchhiking ·47
14 Pound Cake· ·49
15 Roger Spooner, in His Words · · · · · · · · · · · · · · · · ·51
16 Atwood Lane, Nonagenarian · · · · · · · · · · · · · · · · ·64
17 Feed Mills ·68
18 A Visit With Clifford ·71
19 Down-Home Fun· ·73

20	Figs and First Friend ·78
21	Raising the Kids· ·81
22	Gasoline ·83
23	The Pond· ·86
24	Kennith Fields (March 26, 1931 - July 8, 1950) · · · · · · · · ·90
25	Sharecropping· ·94
26	Who Was Paul Raymond Evans? ·98
27	Hard Fall ·103
28	Red Devils and War Eagles ·106
29	Donalsonville Elementary School Food · · · · · · · · · · · · ·108
30	Alf Greene· ·111
31	Barnyards ·117
32	Rolled Over· ·122
33	Tater Bank ·125
34	Where to Put Dessert? ·126

Part II Newer Stuff · **127**

35	Traveling Man ·129
36	Windjammer Barefoot Cruise ·138
37	Close Call ·141
38	Sometimes the Best Intentions· ·143
39	The Travails of Being a "Mister Chef"· · · · · · · · · · · · · · · ·146
40	God Acts in Mysterious Ways· ·148
41	Anatomy of a Scam· ·152
42	Plumbing for Dollars ·154
43	Our Last Picture Show· ·157
44	Hovering Outside the Pearly Gates · · · · · · · · · · · · · · · · · ·159
45	As God Would Have It ·163
46	In Memory of Robert (Pop) Garner Trawick · · · · · · · · · · ·165
47	Prominent ·169
48	Californy Or Bust· ·171
49	Terror on Econfina Creek ·175

Part III Stuff **179**
50 Life 181
51 Locked-Down 183
52 Just Imagine 185
53 Time 187
54 Symbols 189
55 The Pretentious Among Us 191
56 From For-Granted to Precious 193
57 It Went Where? 195
58 What Rattles the Brain 197
59 Alzheimer's 200

Prologue

Experiences and people are the stuff of which life is made. Following is a sharing of old stuff, newer stuff and stuff essays. Four of our senior citizens: Atwood Lane, Roger Spooner, Clifford Cannington, and Alf Greene were generous in passing on their long ago recollections of experiences which mattered to them. For the other stories, the author relied on his memories of stand-out experiences with an emphasis on the '50s, '60s, '70s, and extending to the current year.

Unique among people is that what matters to one person can matter and draw interest from his peers, and therefore the stories shared tend to attract and appeal to all in the rural South. Those individuals passing on information to me certainly captured my interest. The county locals and others can identify with the heritage of Seminole County because it is in many ways their story, their heritage by association.

The "newer stuff" came chiefly from the adventures, misadventures, successes, and disappointments of my life and Connie's. The stuff of life has a generous sprinkling of discombobulations, dents, bangs, trip wires, land mines, delights, harshness, laughs, and "specials" to which we are all susceptible.

The "stuff" portion comprises a collection of observations I have made of life as I have lived my seventy-one years. It is a commentary on life in the raw which I encountered along my journey. By no means is it perfect, but most assuredly it is candid and honest.

Part I Old Stuff

1

Remembrances of Childhood

Following is a compilation of memories from childhood; recollections which are in common with most of my peers:

- Getting an ice cream cone with strawberry, vanilla and chocolate being the only choices
- The scent of new denim on the first day of school
- The feel of a new pair of black and white Keds tennis shoes
- The look of approval Mama gave after carefully reviewing a report card and signing it
- The fun of finally talking Mama into letting me go barefooted in the springtime with the feel of dirt under bare feet
- Going behind the smokehouse to cry after a switching
- A bumpy ride on the tailgate of a pickup truck
- Santa Claus coming to town and kids scrambling for the candy tossed on the street.
- The feeling of excitement and anticipation when walking into a movie on Saturday afternoon
- The taste of the world's best hotdog bought at the theatre concession
- Playing "Red Rover" with classmates
- Watching the girls jump rope with amazement at their skills and "hot peas"
- Getting in a tussle on the playground and learning that there is always someone stronger and more skilled

- The awkwardness of trying to fit into an environment which offered no comfort
- Warily watching the teacher to be the first to confirm the "boiling point"
- The terrifying moment of realization when Mama's patience had depleted
- The morning greeting from Chief with teeth smiling and tail switching
- Backing up to the fire place to take the "outside chill" off
- The warm, secure feeling of being immersed in a feather bed with quilts piled on
- The barely bearable heat and sweat of the cotton patch
- The earthy smell of the peanut fields
- Lifting the lid on the Coke cooler at Hill Pace's service station and pulling out a truly ice cold six-ounce Coke
- Checking the bottom of the Coke bottle to determine which town it came from
- The smells in the air and the feeling of warmth and love in the kitchen as the family sat down to a breakfast of grits, eggs, syrup, biscuits and bacon
- Anxiously sitting around the TV on Saturday nights at 10 o'clock to watch "Gunsmoke"
- The sound of rain on the tin roof as sleep came so easily
- The strange nowhere-else smells of Donalsonville Hospital during a doctor's visit
- The casual banter between doctors Baxley and Jenkins and the feelings of reassurance they gave
- Eating Mama's still warm pound cake with a glass of milk
- Licking the pound cake mixing bowl with finger and tongue
- The taste of sliced tomatoes, butter beans, fresh corn, hoe cakes, fried chicken and egg custard for dessert
- The feeling of clothes totally soaked in sweat as we picked cotton
- Tugging on Mama's dress and wanting to go home when she stopped to visit a relative

Old Stuff, Newer Stuff, and Stuff

- Watching Grandma Mills drink the milk and raw egg each morning and wondering how she could do it
- Racing to the mailbox to check for *The Weekly Reader*
- The large family reunions with good food and good love shared by all
- Staring at the picture of Jesus on the Ingram Funeral Home fan during church
- The warm, homey feeling of the fireplace at Emmet Ward's grocery store
- The pleasant smell of pitch pine when chopping kindling from a pine stump
- The bite of the winter wind when walking to and waiting for the school bus
- Eating oranges, tangerines, pecans and brazil nuts around the crackling fireplace at Christmas time and tossing the debris in the fire
- The taste of Mama's apple sauce fruitcake after fermenting in a lard can with a whisky spike added
- The spread of Mama's food on the table at Thanksgiving and Christmas and the closeness and love of the family enjoying the food and fellowship
- Boarding the school bus in the afternoon to take the long ride home
- The anticipation of all the fun to have during Christmas vacation as school turned out for two weeks
- Ordering a cherry Coke at Roberts Pharmacy
- The warmth of the air and the mixture of essences after a summer rain
- Sitting in the porch swing on the front porch and watching the traffic go by
- Listening to Daddy play his guitar or mandolin on Sunday mornings
- The disappointment of being left behind when my older brothers went hunting
- The anticipation of grades as the teacher returned the test papers

- The huge amount, the savory tastes, and the variety of food on the fifty to sixty foot long table at church on Sundays
- Holding a flashlight while my brother shot wharf rats under the barn with a 22 rifle
- The overhanging, shady, beautiful oaks on HWY 84 through Donalsonville and HWY 45 in Iron City
- Watching fist fights behind the canning plant in high school
- Adding the last touches to homework in the morning before school
- Watching the calf and pig scrambles at the annual cattle show
- Watching the ground carefully for rattlesnakes when trekking the woods hunting quail
- The startle and excitement of a covey of quail flushing
- The clean plate after eating in the school cafeteria and wishing there were more
- The kick of the shotgun and the action of pumping shells into the magazine as the spent ones are ejected
- Seeing a clean kill of a dove in flight as he headed toward the ground and Mama's cooking pot
- Shelling peas and butter beans for hours and hours under a mimosa tree
- The feeling of accomplishment as we hoed the last row of peanuts and walked out of the field
- Pouring slop into the pig trough and watching the swine fight over what they regarded as delicious
- The independent feeling of finally being able to reach items in the upper kitchen cabinets
- The odor of corn soaked in lye for the pigs
- The perfumed fragrance of wisteria on a spring morning
- Mama's look of disappointment when I misbehaved. A look was all it took to bring correction
- The whistle of a train passing through Iron City three miles away
- The cool, delicious, satisfying taste of water from the faucet at the well

- The aroma of parched peanuts wafting from the peanut vendor on the sidewalk
- The beehive of activity and the sounds of people laughing and visiting in Donalsonville on Saturday afternoon
- The amazing amount of curios and items on and in the counters of the Dime Store and the smell of popcorn at the door
- The thrill of getting in the pickup truck on Friday nights to go to town, see friends and play pool
- The surreptitious passing of a note down the row of desks from one friend to another The inevitability of the note tossed across the aisle eventually being seen by the teacher
- The somber moment when the teacher reached in the middle drawer of the desk for the paddle
- The cringe of watching a fellow classmate lean over the desk for a paddling
- The tremendous satisfaction of the last day of high school and the accomplishment of walking away from the principal with a diploma in hand
- The awkwardness of socializing with pretty girls
- The humbling feeling of being in an embarrassing situation
- The anticipation of knowing a future waited out there with exciting possibilities

2

Copperhead Fun

My brother Lloyd loved fun and practical jokes. Whether or not it was at the expense of a friend or relative did not matter. Fun was fun, and he would claim it whenever the opportunity developed; let the consequences fall where they may.

A summer day circa 1980 found him working in a peanut field with his nephew Geno Brown, age about sixteen. Also present was Kojak, Lloyd's faithful bulldog which was always with his master.

As they were quitting work for the day, they heard Kojak barking his head off at something in the grass near a fence. He had found a copperhead about four feet long which started the wheels in Lloyd's devious head turning. While downing his first drink of whiskey right out of the bottle with only fresh air for a chaser, he suggested for Geno to catch the copperhead. Geno did not have to think long before his desire for whatever fun his uncle had in mine overwhelmed his best judgment.

Geno found a board in the back of Lloyd's truck and pinned the copperhead's head so he could get a good grasp on him. Grabbing the snake snugly at the back of his head, he presented the prize to Lloyd for the next step in whatever craziness he had planned.

Lloyd plundered in his truck's tool box and retrieved a pair of pliers. He told Geno to squeeze the snake near the back of his jaws which would cause his mouth to open and the fangs to extend. Lloyd grabbed each fang with the pliers and pulled it out. They had a fangless moccasin that could hurt no one but could scare the hell out of everybody.

During the interim, Kojak had been going crazy watching the snake wiggle while Lloyd and Geno performed their "dental procedure." Kojak, switching his tail and barking wildly, desperately wanted a piece of the action.

Lloyd instructed Geno to place the moccasin on the ground to see what Kojak would do with this wiggling reptile. Kojak had dealt with snakes before and had earned a large measure of respect for slithering reptiles. Whatever involvement he had with this guy was going to be with a huge dose of caution.

A loudly barking Kojak approached the snake, and the snake struck at him causing Kojak to jump about three feet high and backward at the same time. Kojak's natural instincts told him he did not want the serpent touching him, but the dog in him and his master's urging said he had a job to do, and he needed to "have it out" with the snake.

In his previous encounters with slithering beasts, none had been extremely poisonous, or he would not have been in this fight. He carried the utmost concern for the lightening moves and wily strikes of his opponent.

Again, Kojak circled the copperhead, drawing closer to tempt the crawler. His presence enraged the snake who was already in a bad mood from the unscheduled "visit with the dentist" a few minutes ago. The copperhead instinctively wanted to sink his "missing fangs" into the barking wonder.

The snake grew smarter and held his motion until Kojak finally got close enough for contact. With a lightening strike, he plowed into the dog's nose with a loud thump. He yelped loudly and back flipped realizing he had a very worthy opponent. Where did that punch come from?

This bout had become outrageous and laugh-out-loud funny for the guys. During this action, Lloyd and Geno had been bellowing with laughter. The first drink of whiskey had hit its mark, so Lloyd's world became a funnier, livelier place. They laughed until their stomachs hurt. They knew Kojak enjoyed taking on anything that came along including rabbits, possums, skunks, snakes and rats. Today he was bewildered in that he did not know what to do exactly with Mr. Copperhead, especially after the strong jab landed on his nose.

With the sun almost setting, the time for the end-of-the-day ritual of heading to Larry's bar in Iron City to drink and carouse with buddies had arrived. Lloyd told Geno to put the copperhead in an empty fish cooler in the back of his truck. Not seeming to be a strange request to Geno, he fully suspected the fun to be had with the fangless reptile was not nearly over.

Driving to Iron City and entering the bar, Lloyd ordered a glass of ice to go with his Lord Calvert. It was time to praise the Lord. Gene enjoyed a Coca Cola. Late in the afternoon and early evening the room was crowded as usual with hard-working men enjoying the camaraderie, fresh tales, favorite beverages, and dominos or pool.

Lloyd's cousin Walter Spooner was there as usual doing his thing and laughing loudly with his friends.

Knowing Walter well, Lloyd possessed two pieces of information that he could use to give Walter a hard time and everyone else a good laugh: Walter hated snakes with extreme passion and loved fish.

Lloyd told Walter that he had a cooler full of fish in the back of the truck, and he was welcome to a mess of them. He suggested grabbing a bucket from the truck and filling it up. Being time for Walter to check out, Lloyd and Geno gathered around the window of the bar and urged others to join them as Walter walked out to the truck.

Walter quickly and nonchalantly flipped back the cooler lid and confronted one-more-pissed-off copperhead which struck in the direction of his face. Walter instinctively jumped backward and screamed so loud it could have been heard at Rock Pond, three miles away. He took off running while swinging his arms and circled the bar building yelling.

The men in the bar were laughing so hard they were spilling drinks while they bent over. Lloyd and Geno were leading the laughs because the perpetrators always "got it" more than the bystanders. The noise in the bar reached a deafening crescendo.

Lloyd and Geno shuffled outside to see where Walter had gone and found him huffing and puffing as he came from behind the bar. Needless to say Walter was none too happy with them and uttered language for which his daddy would not be proud. Opening fish coolers would not be the same for the rest of his life, and he may have lost his taste for fish.

So went another hard-working, hard-drinking day for men of the earth. Having experienced a day that those In New York City could not imagine, they had enjoyed life to the fullest and the outrageously funny antics that came with it—in their world.

3

Alma Adams

Miss Alma, aka Aunt Alma Adams

She could have been equally comfortable teaching in a one-room school house at the turn of the twentieth century as at Seminole County High School. Constructed of the same stuff from which toughness is made, she was capable of handling anything which came her way. Life did not push her around. She pushed it around.

Not knowing who she was, I had become familiar with Miss Alma long before sitting in her Algebra I class. With her being a member of Olive Grove Primitive Baptist Church in the Rock Pond community, I had often seen her at church when I went with Mama. She lived her religion as she lived the rest of her life with full-bore conviction in her actions, blunt words, and commitment to her beliefs.

Not only a church member, she was regarded as a member of our extended family. John E. Adams had married Mama's sister Edna so all the Adams were like family. Alma's relatives, John Quincy and Sweetzer Adams, were elders in the church. The church in those days had a way of cementing relationships in the family of the Lord.

The fall of 1959 found me sitting in Miss Alma's Algebra One class along with twenty-five or thirty other ambitious math students. With Algebra being a step or two beyond eighth grade math, students were required to think more abstractly. Miss Alma with all her teaching acumen had a way of laying it out which I understood. Looking around the room at sad faces and hearing people moan about their marked up red test papers assured me fellow classmates were in a mathematical fog and could remain not understanding "X" in front of their faces or a "Y."

Miss Alma was a no-nonsense teacher who gave no quarter to misbehaving slackers. Choosing to whisper to a buddy carried a great risk of having to bend over her desk while she got exercise, and a rule-breaker developed a case of "touchous butt."

Her strong religious beliefs could bring forth a five-minute sermon on life in quick order. Having no inclination to understand students' personalities and idiosyncrasies, they adapted to her rather than she accommodate their weaknesses. She espoused "religion according to Miss Alma" and assured everyone, "Your sins will find you out." Those who found themselves leaning across her desk had their sins well exposed.

She would also sermonize on life and why we all should be listening and learning. Miss Alma warned of the hard, cruel world we would one day confront and wanted us to be prepared. She was so right as we all later plunged into a sink-or-swim world, we could not have anticipated.

Mama said that Miss Alma had gotten TB of the hip bone in her earlier life which explained her limp. The misfortune did not slow her down in my observation. She could be seen hustling down the hall at top speed "on a mission" daily.

She was quick of mind, so trying to BS her was a conspicuous waste of time. Thinking several steps ahead of whoever might be trying to hoodoo her or attempting to spin her top brought no rewards. The mental contest was over before it started.

Miss Alma, one of the teachers who was the face of SCHS for many years, shares a cherished place in the minds of her students, even the "sinners." Strong in character and determined of will, she was a certified original to whom many students owe gratitude and pleasant reminiscences.

Rest in peace, Miss Alma. You left us a heritage of good memories, a knowledge of mathematics, and an appreciation for doing the right things or facing the consequences when sins find us out.

4

A Changing Landscape

In the Seminole County farming community of the early fifties, tractor farming was rapidly replacing mule farming. There were tractors in the county in the forties, but the era was the proving ground. By today's standards the early tractors were archaic and cumbersome as was the equipment which accompanied them.

Uncle Howard's John Deere tractor was the first tractor I had seen. The motor seemed to chug and cough when compared to today's smooth running engines and to a novice seemed about to choke down. It was Daddy's first exposure to hands-on mechanized farming.

Starting an old John Deere with a hand crank on a cold morning could be a foreboding task. After the addition of electric starters, a hand crank backup facility remained on most tractors. When cranking our Farmall with a hand crank because the battery was weak, I had to be really careful to pull the crank out quickly as I spun the engine, or it would start rotating with the motor and possibly break something near and dear, an arm or leg.

The steering mechanism was stiff, cumbersome with loose motion and no power steering. Rotating the steering wheel required substantial muscle especially on sharp turns. Close plowing of the rows of crops was a skill that only the best drivers such as Daddy had fully mastered. Valuable crop plants could be plowed up in an instant with a small drifting from row alignment.

There were two kinds of people: city dwellers and country folks. If you did not farm, you lived in town. If you farmed, you lived in the country.

This may sound elementary, but when one contrasts it with today, many people living in the country have nothing to do with farming. They simply prefer to or are comfortable with living outside of the city.

Seminole Countians who lived in the country owned farms, usually passed at least partially from another generation, and made the land their source of income. Very few people other than older, retired farmers and wives lived in the country and did not farm.

My memory has retained the name of every farmer in or adjacent to the Rock Pond community as well as many outside of the area. A tour of the area reveals that on today's Tom and Brandy Trawick Road there were three farm families: Tom Trawick's, Brandy's, and Earl Ward's. Junior Bowen, a WWII veteran, lived and farmed on the cutoff road between the Tom/Brand Road and Three Notch Road.

Coming out of Iron City on Three Notch Road, Marsden Strickland's farm blanketed both sides of the Road. Marsden had the rare distinction of being a farmer who lived in town. His land was adjacent to his house in Iron City, so it was almost like living on his farm. About a quarter mile up the road from Iron City, Enoch Ausley had a farm bordering the right side of the road. Going south past Marsden's property on the left was Ralph and Hardy Horne's land. Adjacent to them on the left was my Uncle Denmark and Aunt Ollie Godby Trawick's farm.

Anderson Williams' farm was next going south from Rock Pond. Mrs. Waver Love had land on the right south of Anderson. Going south of Waver, George and Rosa Mae Trawick, with whom Daddy sharecropped in the later '50s, had their farm.

Going east of Rock Pond was Miller Town with many farm families: Drew, Harvey, HE, Calvin, and others that have left my memory.

Proceeding west of Rock Pond was more Marsden Strickland land on the right. George Odom (Raymond's father) purchased Strickland's farm in the mid-fifties. Next going west on the left side of the road was the Mills's farm. On the right side of the road was the Bud and Lila Mae Youmans's farm.

Adjacent to the Youmans's farm on the right was my great uncle Gordon Spooner's property a portion of which we sharecropped my last few years of high school. In that time period Raymond Simmons and his wife Nettie Doris Spooner Simmons (Gordon's daughter) had assumed ownership of the farm.

Across the road from Gordon's land was the farm of my great uncle Luke and Aunt Delia Jernigan Spooner. The property was the home place of my great granddaddy Joe Spooner where he raised his family. Circa 1950 Uncle Luke tore down the old home and built him and Delia a smaller home with the lumber. In the fifties Luke had quit farming and only raised cattle leaving his son Billy to farm the land.

Next door to Gordon's land and on the west side of Spooner Road was my great uncle Howard's farm. About three-fourths mile further down the road on the left was the beautiful home and land of Bartow and Euna Spooner Gibson. Bartow raised a quantity of cattle, but rented his cultivatable land. Quite the entrepreneur of the day, Bartow owned Gibson Construction, Roadside Milling and a few thousand acres of land.

On the left adjacent to Bartow and the other side of Fish Pond Drain was a farm held by an African American whose last name was Hunter if my memory holds. He owned seventy-five acres plus of cultivated land which Jabo King bought and developed Arrowhead Estates. Jabo did well with his vision of turning the farm field into a beautiful, desired community in which to live.

When we travel up Spooner Road going north from Gibson Road, we encounter many farm families of yesterday. First on the left was Ray and Mary Jane Lane Spooner's land. Past it on the left was my great uncle Carl and Lola Spooner's land. Across the road from Carl, Frank and Cordelia Spooner had land which he rented as he got on in years.

On the left going north was Otis Brackin's farm. TE Roberts had land on both sides of the road north of Otis. Ralph Dozier had land across the road from Otis.

As a tribute to the farmers of the era, a portion of their names follow: Byron Cobb, Les Kidd, Ralph Trawick, Phil Spooner, Joe Spooner, Rudolph Spooner, Luther Spooner, Eddie Kelly, John Cummings, Tom Miller, Roy Mims, Earl Mims, Ned Alday, Aubrey Alday, Roy Faircloth, Ed

Hand, Lewis Roberts, Sampson Waddell, Marsett Waddell, Al Cordell, Slim Ausley, HR Dozier, Bill Dozier, Booge Roberts, Eldridge Hornsby, Clarence Hornsby, Melvin Hornsby, Royce Hornsby, Morris Hornsby, Frank Braswell, Fred Ingram, Sam Frazier, Jake Lane, Jack Burke, Sylvester Burke, Arthur Bramlett, Truett Roberts, and many others my memory has lost.

These great farmers of the fifties have passed except for Bud Youmans, a living institution. Born with dirt beneath their fingers, they were so blessed to have lived the simpler life in the best of times when a man's word was as good as gold. Doing their very best with what they worked with, all were remarkable contributors to the county, their communities, and their families.

Those who farmed loved the earth and the independence of managing one's own business. From their fathers and their fathers' fathers, genes had been passed which made them "worship" land ownership and the benefits which came with it. The successful farmers refused to allow the possibility of selling land to enter their minds. Buying more property to expand their operations, they saw as the only option.

Land proved to be a wise investment. When my daddy sold his fifty acres for $25,000 including the house circa 1969, he received $500 per acre. Today irrigated farm land can bring as much as $6,000 per acre and will only appreciate in value. In the next twelve years prices could move to $10,000 per acre or greater as competition for the value of the land and water beneath heats up.

A careful observer can witness more and more forest land being cleared for crop production. "Truck crops" such as carrots and potatoes continue to be harvested in increasing quantities. "Futurists" predict more and more crop trucks being farmed in the sandy loam soil of Seminole County with its tremendous underground water supply.

Seminole County rests on one of the best underground water supplies in the country and possibly the world. The huge amount of water flowing through the Chattahoochee, Flint Rivers and Spring Creek could only be dwarfed by two huge aquifers beneath the county.

Since the '60s, the small family operations have disappeared, yielding to huge family farms, corporate farms, and farms owned by insurance companies, which are rented to large farm producers. Economies of volume, the efficiencies of modern farm equipment, and product pricing have made this possible. Unintentionally, federal subsidies have also made a contribution to this evolution.

5

Old Spring Creek Power Dam

Circa 1952 Mama, Daddy, I, and occasionally my two brothers would go to the power dam on Spring Creek to fish. It was one heck of a treat, at least to me. Mama would pack a lunch for a most-of-the-day outing, and we would have a picnic under the trees about twenty-five to thirty yards up the west bank.

About a hundred yards from the dam sat Ottie Morris' store with the "grab all" goodies including bait found in a country store. It had charm all its own, but not as well-stocked as Goree's. Never having to buy bait since we grunted our own pond worms from a swampy, wooded area near our house, we purchased tackle and limited sundries. Store-bought goodies were avoided.

The store's proprietor played an unfortunate role in the history of the time. Ottie Morris shot Cliff Whittaker as Cliff drove up to Ottie's house. They had differences causing Ottie to step out of the bushes and shoot him after Cliff had apparently threatened Ottie a few minutes before.

Late in 2016 I visited with a nephew of Ottie Morris who filled in details of the shooting of which I had not been familiar. Mr. Morris came into Sunny's Deli and had lunch with Connie and I after we introduced ourselves.

Cliff had rental cabins and a restaurant located behind Ottie's store which catered to fishermen. Animosity had been brewing between the two for an extended period of time. Rumors indicated that a shared girl friend could have been at the crux of the conflict. The relationship was ripe for a breaking point when they had words at Cliff's restaurant that morning regarding an unknown subject. When Cliff reportedly said he was going to kill Ottie, their fate was sealed.

Cliff was in his jeep and drove up to Ottie's house when Ottie fired at him with a shot gun and a pellet also struck his son Bunky Whittaker who was riding in the vehicle. What a terrible experience for a young child!

A trial followed, and Ottie was not convicted with the verbal threat playing a crucial part in the verdict.

The story made an impression on me since it was the first local murder I had experienced. It bothered Mama and Daddy causing them to talk about it extensively with me actively listening. Death by homicide was foreign to the county.

Mr. Morris shared another interesting story about a bear Ottie had in a cage behind the store. Morris being a young tike of five or six at the time would offer his Nehi orange to the bear through the cage wire. To Ottie's dismay he walked back to check on the kid one day and found him in the cage with the bear sharing his drink. An unnerved Ottie jerked the kid out of the cage and quickly padlocked it.

People could fish in only in a few places at the power dam: on the concrete landing, which the water ran under, along the west bank, or on the railroad trestle which trains no longer used. The dam still generated electricity at the time. I preferred being on the large concrete walkway with the noisy sound of the water and the violent flow. People would sit on the edge of the concrete and fish in the water below.

At six to eight years old, lacking the technique and the patience to fish, I watched while others caught them and waded in the shallows near the bank. Mama always tired quickly of repairing my line.

When someone loaned Daddy a boat, we fished thirty or forty yards downstream of the dam, Daddy dropped a huge iron anchor to keep the boat positioned in the churning water. A big redbelly he landed was the largest bream I had ever seen. Mama caught a few, but with me trying hard my catch amounted to diddle,

On a Saturday twenty to forty people would populate the dam, along the banks and the trestle. Occasionally during the week if it were too wet to work in the fields, a crowd would come to fish. The dam was one of those places where country people congregated, visited, and had an enjoyable time in nature.

The closing of the dam coincided with the Jim Woodruff power plant completion. Soon after the startup, three fishermen became the first drowned in the Lake Seminole. An Odom, a Daniels and a gentleman from out of town were the unfortunate. The loss weighed hard on the county as the recovery effort of "dragging" the lake went on for several days before finding the bodies.

When I drive by the old power dam today, I try to imagine the scene and the activities of the time. Gone is another portion of Seminole County history, but the structure still stands as a tribute to pleasant, fun days and times gone by.

6

What I Miss About Donalsonville

As I think about the Donalsonville of the '50s and early '60s, a potpourri of visions come into mind; special memories which are held dearly. The quaint little farm town had it all. The scenes, events, and day to day living experiences were genuine and played out by good, honest people in this typical, rural Americana town. The many recollections which stand out in my memory follow:

<u>Beautiful oak trees along Hwy. 84.</u> Perhaps the strongest and most nostalgic memory, the trees overlapping the two lane highway defined the town and added irreplaceable beauty and charm. Covering both sides and the middle of the two lane street pretty much from the present day location of Dollar General to the Methodist Church, they provided a shaded canopy below which traveler's passed.

In the name of progress, this "picture postcard" of the town's personality was sacrificed in about the mid '50s. A place on the road to Marianna where the oak trees grow across the road and meet causes me to reminisce of those long gone works of nature's art.

<u>Crowds of people on the downtown sidewalks on Saturday.</u> Farm people who were busy all week found time on Saturdays to come to town, shop, and visit with their friends. Socializing required as much or more time as shopping. Buying groceries was the main focus, but money was spent at all the local retailers dependent on the patrons' needs of the moment. Doing well financially with the huge traffic, retailers flourished.

The sidewalks provided a platform for extensive palavering. A couple of people would stop and visit with others joining in causing the group to grow. The obstruction of sidewalk traffic could become unwieldy, but no one really complained. Pedestrians understood the great spirit and love of people, so they found a way through or around the "social circles."

The people traffic had its preferences of location. The multitudes seemed always to congregate on the sidewalk along Dismukes, the Surprise Store, Andrew Lynn's and City Grocery. Brown stains from tobacco and snuff spit would decorate the sidewalks. With essentially all parking places taken, hundreds of people owned the sidewalks and enjoyed the fun. If a family found a reasonably close parking place, they did not move the vehicle to find a better one, or they would be driving around for a while.

Mama used to run into a Mr. Bush, who always wore overalls. Every time she would greet him by saying, "Hey, Old Crazy." They would chat for a minute and do the same thing the next time they saw each other. Walking with Mama taught me how everyone seemed to know a lot of people, a huge benefit and joy of small towns.

<u>The Saturday matinees at the two theaters: the Peoples and the Dunn.</u> Kids went to the "show" while Mom and Pop shopped and visited. Donald Duck, Porky Pig, Bugs Bunny, Woody Woodpecker, Wiley Coyote, Yosemite Sam and other cartoons shown with the main cowboy feature proved to be a winning combination. The show was very popular and drew large crowds of young people on Saturday afternoons. Sometimes with the theater being almost filled, I would have to walk around for a minute to find a seat. After the older kids got the courage to hold hands during the movie, they may have claimed to be boy friends and girl friends.

<u>Green Top Motel and Cafe.</u> Frank and Ruby Rachel had the go-to place for burgers and hanging out in the '50s. They owned about ten motel rooms, and a cafe that was noted to have the best burgers in the area. With the juke box blasting the tunes of the day and the booths filled, the place pulled in the traffic. Both young and old patronized the business.

<u>Mills Rexall Drug Store.</u> Dr. Mills was in his later years when I first became acquainted. I remember the boney, arthritic fingers grasping a bottle of pills or liquid. I don't know when his business started but suspect he was a key member of the town's merchandisers for a long time.

He exuded a kind, dependable, caring demeanor. My mother took a liquid blood pressure medicine, dark in color which he mixed while we waited. In one instance Daddy drove to his house and got him to come to the pharmacy to fill a much needed prescription, an accommodation not to be found today.

When I contracted the "ground itch," he sold a can of obnoxious spray to freeze the parasite which kids got by going barefoot. Dr. Mills could easily see the raised worm-like portion of skin where it resided. The freezing from the spray can brought terrible pain. Baby doll tears gushed, but at the moment the crying seemed worthy of stopping the terrible itching. Occasionally a dreaded second treatment was necessary, and they had to run me down for a replay of the torture.

Jitney Jungle. Lonnie Jernigan owned the first grocery store of size in town. J. Lonnie, always friendly, always helpful, and with an infectious laugh, had the perfect temperament for the job it seemed. We would have extra vegetables from our farm which he would buy. Unloading bushel baskets of black eyed peas, snap beans and butter beans at the back of the store was not uncommon for any farmer.

At five years old, wondering through the store aisles with the huge assortment of groceries was a special treat. Where did all the stuff come from? How did it get here? Until then I had only seen Emmett Ward's small grocery.

Lois's Cafe. Next door, west of the Julian Webb house stood Lois Doster's Cafe. If a patron wanted a sit down meal be it breakfast, lunch, or supper, it was the place to go. Their broasted chicken, coated with crumbs and baked in an oven, was my only experience from Lois. Mama would infrequently get a box to go on Saturday night supper to save her from having to cook. It could not quite compete with her fried chicken but was a delicious treat.

Being served a full sit-down meal in a Donalsonville restaurant, our family could not afford. We ate Mama's cooking at home.

The Surprise Store. Earl Wilson was the manager, and Jabo King served as his right hand man. When the time came to start back to school, The Surprise Store is where we bought new shoes. Jabo had a knack for gab and making people feel comfortable; even little ten year old kids. He could quickly grab a couple of boxes of shoes out of the back room and fit them on me with a pleasant demeanor. Jeans and new shirts were also available for the back-to-school shopper. As local history evolved, Jabo, moved way beyond a store clerk position, grew in his entrepreneurship, and did well as a local businessman.

Bivings. The nicer back to school clothing could be found at Bivings. Loads of inventory filled the shelves and tables. Genuinely friendly, helpful salespeople knew the shopper and could help him or her find what was wanted. Fellow classmates, working there on Saturdays or after school, could be the ones serving the school patrons.

The store provided a foot x-ray machine, a popular novelty with young customers, on which a patron could stand to see how well their feet fit in shoes. As the harmful nature of excessive x-raying became known, the owners removed the machine.

Roberts Pharmacy. With an old fashioned soda fountain and counter with lots of polished chrome, Yank Roberts' business had a personality all its own. Having the distinction of being the only place downtown, other than Mills' Rexall Drugs, where people could get a cherry coke, it had a special attraction. A funny book stand with a generous amount of offerings for the time stood near the front door. Once Yank yanked my chain when he asked for a penny tax on a ten cent funny book. He let me have it any way after he had his fun. Ten cents was all I had. Yes, they were funny books to locals, not comic books. Not sure Yank knew how to smile.

Thomas' Five and Ten. The Thomas brothers, Ross and Taylor, thrived for a number of years with Thomas Five and Ten Cent, or the Dime Store. The glass counters filled with a huge variety of "what-have-yous" fascinated small children. The large quantity of items for five or ten cents pulled in the adult customers. Linda Faye Worthington staffed the bulk candy counter. She would scoop your choice of jellybeans, chocolate covered peanuts, and other sweet delights and deposit it in a white paper bag. Popcorn could be purchased just outside the front door.

Harry King's Barber Shop. Harry, his brother Newton, and George Walden staffed a barbershop adjacent to Rabon Furniture Store. In my family hair was cut on Saturdays as was the custom with most farm families. With hordes of people in town, the barbers had all the business they needed. It was quite common for approximately ten chairs for waiting to be filled to capacity.

If a customer wanted a shoe shine, "Shine" could provide it. In a few minutes a patron could practically see his face in his shoes.

Shine always started with a little soapy water and a small brush with which he cleaned the shoes. Then he wiped them with a cloth. He applied polish with his bare hands and finished with his shine cloth moving back and forth in a blur and an occasional popping of it as he jerked it fast. Twenty-five cents paid directly to Shine bought a shoeshine.

Harry, Newton, and George always had their conversations going covering the weather, local news, politics, and whatever came up. Sitting in their chairs and not getting brought into a conversation proved impossible for their customers.

<u>Hardy's Barber Shop.</u> As I got older, I gravitated to Hardy's for haircuts. My brother knew where to get a cool hair cut, so I followed. Mrs. Hardy would cut hair like the customer wanted it, in contrast to Harry's where there was one cut, skin the sides and take a little off of the top. Mr. Hardy, a side-skinner, had my business only when Miss Flo was backed up.

<u>Rabon Furniture.</u> Melton and Lois Rabon owned the only furniture store in town for many years. When we could afford new furniture, it came from Rabon Furniture. Of course our furniture purchases were few and way far between. Being well-liked and trusted in the community, customers including my parents, regarded them as friends.

Melton delivered to our house a dining table and chairs, the nicest pieces we had owned. They replaced an old wooden table with two long benches and a chair at each end.

Showing Mama and Daddy how to sit in the chairs, he advised them they were made to sit in squarely and cautioned them to not lean back as in a rocking chair, or they would weaken and need repair; sound advice for his customers.

Can we imagine the proprietor of a furniture store today delivering furniture?

<u>The Tastee Freeze.</u> Circa 1960 Doc Sheffield constructed and opened the Tastee Freeze across the street from the high school with his wife Mercedes as the manager.

Its popularity made everyone wonder what kids did before it arrived. The Tastee Freeze had it all: a huge parking lot, a new building with an abundance of glass in the front, a juke box that blared songs into the parking area, good food/drinks, booths, and Mercedes doing a fine job of directing operations.

If teenagers with a driver permit went to town, they spent at least part of their time in the restaurant or in the parking lot shooting the breeze with their friends. Talking through windows to each other often varied with a group of friends standing in a crowd in the parking lot. Many a long relationship was started and nourished at the Tastee Freeze. On football and basketball home game nights, the place was a sea of cars and activity with scant parking places.

Michael Whittle "car-hopped" and will be remembered by the teenagers of the period. He did not forget anything. Michael had the memory of a genius, which he was. Writing down orders usually proved unnecessary for him.

After high school, Michael earned a medical degree and became a pathologist, making his home in Tennessee.

When we had classes on the southern end of the high school in the afternoon, the class could hear the juke box going across the street. I can still almost hear "Up on the Roof" and "Walk Right In" which were popular in 1963.

<u>City Grocery/Piggly Wiggly.</u> Through working hard and managing well, Hoyt Newberry and his brother Horace brought a new dimension to the grocery business. They started in the business with City Grocery which was small and jam-packed on Saturdays.

In a few years Hoyt had left Horace to run it while he opened a new-construction Piggly Wiggly where Harvey's eventually located their business until late 2016. Hoyt and his wife built a strong business which survived and flourished until his passing.

<u>Woodies</u> This restaurant owned and operated by Woodie King was for many years a mainstay in downtown for oysters on the half shell, seafood, and sandwiches. I was not fortunate enough to patronize the place other than walking in briefly, but Daddy would find an opportunity to visit late Saturday afternoons and partake of a dozen oysters on the half shell. My school friends bragged on the hamburgers.

<u>Jay Rathel's Seafood</u> The business was adjacent to the old high school, on the right side of the Marianna HWY where it forked from HWY 39, and across from where the old agriculture building stood. Only about three hundred fifty square feet encompassed the store's entire space. Free advertisement circulated down the street and could not be ignored, especially when the patrons entered the business which had a strong fish smell.

We would stop there on Saturdays on the way home and buy mullet which Mama would fry or a small can of oysters for stew. Jay would wrap seafood in newspaper when available; otherwise he used "costly" wrapping paper. The practice of wrapping fish in newspaper was highlighted when Lester Maddox ran for governor and referred to the Atlanta Journal and Constitution as the "fish wrapper."

Today I love and eat all fish because I mastered mullet at an early age. For the fish novices, mullet inherently has a strong fish smell and can have an extraordinarily strong fish taste if not really fresh. Daddy, being good friends with Jay and having known him for several years, knew he was buying fresh mullet.

There were many other establishments that could be remembered from Donalsonville's glory days, but these are highlights of memories from places where I had an association.

The effort to rebuild the small "police station" brings back the importance of history. Laws regarding the uses of four-lane road rights-of-way prevented new oaks from being planted along the paved US 84, along with the problem of tree roots buckling the road. Will the downtown sidewalks be filled again? The warm, friendly town had its heyday, probably never to return again with such bustle.

7

The Smokehouse

Before refrigeration, the curing of meat was critical to supplying adequate protein in the diet. In our country in approximately the early 1700s, smokehouses started appearing as a means of curing and storing precious meat, mostly pork. Over the next couple hundred years, they had extensive use and were critical to ensure meat in the diet year round.

Salt was instrumental in the curing process followed by smoking to dry it out and retard spoilage. The water in the meat facilitated rot and mold, so it had to be removed slowly with smoke over a period of weeks.

Salt and smoking with various techniques were the methods of curing meat until liquid meat cures began emerging in the 1900s. The best liquid cure was Figaro which was patented on, December 5, 1950, and has lasted until present day.

Those who read *Syrup, Biscuits and Sow Belly* may remember my curiosity of why ours was called a smokehouse when no smoking went on in my day. After doing research, I figured out why the dirt-floor structure bore the term smokehouse.

Prior to my birth, the structure was used to smoke meat as its name suggests. In Grandfather Mills' day and Daddy's earlier life, it was used as intended.

The meat was cut, salted, and placed on green pine tops for several days to start the water dripping. Getting the water dripping was the first step in removing all the water.

In the next step they hung the meat in the smokehouse to be smoked and dried. The family built a small fire with green hickory on the dirt floor in the middle of the smokehouse which they kept burning for several weeks until the meat quit dripping.

After the curing, they washed the meat, sliced it, and placed it in metal cans pouring cool lard over each layer to prevent spoiling. The sausage was placed in separate cans and treated similarly.

The old smokehouse that sat about eight or ten steps from our back porch for decades before my time must have had countless secrets locked away. It withstood the storms, heard the family stories, witnessed the hog killings, and provided sanctuary for delicious pork.

The building was about twelve feet square with wooden clapboard siding and a sharply pitched, wood-shingled roof which helped hold the smoke during the curing process. Two by eight cross beams about six feet from the dirt floor supported the curing pieces of meat.

Starting at about five years old, I began developing a vivid picture of the building and its current uses. An enclosed side shed attached to the west side of the building provided Grandma Mills with storage for her preserves and other items. I remember the lines of jars containing pear and peach preserves produced by Grandma still neatly on shelves that eventually had to be discarded because of aging of the contents. Mama stored preserves there for a few years until deterioration finally made it necessary to tear down the shed.

On the east side of the smokehouse was an unusually high table that was only about thirty inches wide. It was built high to preserve the backs of those cutting up swine during hog killing time and measured about ten or twelve feet long. Judging from the age of the boards, I estimated the table was constructed at least twenty years before.

The back side of the structure had an open tin shed under which Mama washed clothes with a scrub board until she got a washing machine in the mid-fifties. Our summertime showers, with a water hose and a Clabber Girl baking powder can with holes in its bottom, were taken under this structure. We always ran to the house with only a towel to find clean clothes.

In my first meat processing memories Daddy used Figaro to greatly simplify the swine curing process. Brushing the liquid generously on the meat and hanging it on the rafters preserved it for some good eating in about six weeks. Figaro retarded spoilage and kept away insects to an extent. Slowly the meat dried in absence of a fire.

We killed hogs and cured meat in the smokehouse until about 1953 when Daddy bought an electric refrigerator. He paid to store our uncured meat in freezer lockers at the Atlantic Coal and Ice Company in Donalsonville for a few years until he bought a chest type freezer to store meat and vegetables.

The old smokehouse was torn down in 1964 when Daddy prepared to build a house in the space where it stood.

Thanks be to Mary Spooner Phillips who published a voluminous book on the Spooner Family. The stories of her early life included a good description of how meat was cured.

8

Solie

My great uncle Howard Spooner and his wife Annie were part of an unlikely situation for their time, or for any time. In my later years I can more fully appreciate the unusual circumstances.

From the time Mama and I would go to visit Uncle Howard and Aunt Annie and for a long period until Aunt Annie's death, a black lady named Solie lived in their house. I have no information of how long she had been living with them though I know it was longer than a decade.

The couple had not been fortunate to have kids, so this lady came to live with them and was virtually one of the family. She was a friendly old soul who was always present and would join the conversation when she was asked a question or wanted to make a comment. She did not have volumes to say.

Tall with a skinny frame of about five feet ten inches or taller, at five years old, when I stood next to her she dwarfed me. I would guess her age was about sixty when I first met her in the early '50s.

Solie loved to dip snuff and often could be found with her can of Sweet Peach and a little frazzle-ended stick from a gum tree that she used to work the snuff around in her mouth. Her teeth had long ago disappeared. I still have a vision of her standing on the edge of the porch and sending a stream all the way to the iron fence that surrounded the Spooner's yard, about ten or twelve feet. She had a deadly aim as well. It was not uncommon to see a dragon fly perched on a bush decimated in a whoosh of snuff spit. Not a pleasant way to go.

In circa 1962 when in my late teen years, I was helping my cousin Luther Spooner haul hay at their farm west of Donalsonville. I had the pleasure of meeting a gentleman, Solie's son, who worked for Luther and was helping with the hay. I was amazed since I had no knowledge of her having a son. His name was Philmore, a friendly hard-working fellow about thirty-five to forty years old.

I can make an educated guess as to how Solie ended up with Uncle Howard and Aunt Annie. Wade Spooner related that her son was raised in a sharecropper house across the road from Ray and Mary Jane Spooner's house. I remember what was left of the house that was deteriorating beside a big oak tree. Probably when Philmore was old enough to leave home, Solie moved in with the Spooners during the Depression.

Uncle Howard passed on at Moseley's Hospital when I was about ten or twelve years old. Mama loved Aunt Annie and him dearly, and I had accompanied her to check on his condition the night he died. Having a problem with alcohol and lying outside on the ground during cold weather contributed to his catching pneumonia.

I remember vividly catching a glimpse of him, propped up in his bed, through his room door when everyone gathered around him as he went on to meet his Maker. Mama was so sad on the trip back home.

Aunt Annie died circa the '70s, and Solie moved to live in a "Sinclair Shingler metal house" in her son's back yard in Donalsonville on seventh street in Porterville. I have no information of when she passed. Before Aunt Annie died, she sold her farm to Will and Gordon Trawick who later sold it to Ray Spooner. I am not sure who owns it today.

A gentleman named John Miller appreciated the beauty of the house and its wrap-around porch on which I used to play. He bought it and had it moved down the road near Fish Pond Drain where he remodeled it and made it his family's home. Melvin and Kathy Lynn Fox restored it to its present day condition. My cousin Judy Youmans Trulock and family live in it today.

9

Fishing

The human species has been eating fish since the cave people. Having no line and hook, getting fish in those days was a problem of survival of the prehistoric families. Moving forward a few millennia, the practice of fishing has taken on an entirely different meaning.

In Seminole County locals celebrate fishing in either of three ways: catching them, eating them, or both. The love of our native fish: bream, shellcrackers, bass, speckled perch (or crappie), and channel catfish still brings eager anticipation. Pulling together a fishing party or an eating party are highlights of the enjoyment of life, fellowship, and nature.

Growing up in this wonderful community, early in life I learned to appreciate all aspects of fishing. At five years old it was fun to go worm grunting. The pond worms would quickly come pouring from the earth, so I would run about gathering them like Easter eggs. That mournful, rhythmic sound of ax head rubbing against a stick driven in the ground still rings in my ears lo these many years later.

Probably I wet my first hook at the Ox Hole on Spring Creek a hundred yards north of the Brinson Bridge. How the deep spot got the name remains a mystery. One can guess that oxen were used for farming in early Georgia history, but to transfer the name of that beast to a fishing hole remains a question mark.

Our "tackle box," which Daddy kept, was always a paper bag with a spool of line, packages of hooks and split shot, and a few "real-cork" corks. Corks made of artificial materials were seldom seen.

Not owning a boat, Mama, Daddy and I would fish from the bank. At least Mama and Daddy fished while I explored the banks and tangled my line into a nice looking bird's nest which could win a prize at the county fair. It seems we only caught but a few, but they all counted in feeding the family.

Occasionally we would come across a highly skilled fisherman like Emmett Braswell who would pull his "string" of fish out of the water and display them proudly as we stood in wonderment. Emmet, a friendly, grizzled, crusty old gentleman, could catch fish in a mud hole, and everyone knew it; those who met him did not forget a genuine character.

From age sixteen until age fifty-nine, I did not fish. Other priorities filled my life, and the opportunity was not available. Around 2001 I started back slowly and accelerated in 2007 with a fierce devotion. Fishing, taking on drug-like characteristics became my addiction, which could have caused me to mainline it right into a vein. I tried to make up for all the lost time, but fruitlessly, impossibly since time can only be used once.

Today with the "putting-food-on-the-table" fixation largely behind us, why do people fish? Visiting this subject in my mind on many occasions, I deduced it has a similar attraction to looking for that toy in the bottom of a box of cracker jacks. Each time the cork sinks and a connection is made, the question becomes, "What will I get this time?" We don't know until we pull it to the top of the water. Hopefully it will be one of the prime eating fish, but occasionally our hearts sink as we pull out a sharp-toothed gar, an eel, a black fish, a carp, or a shad. Back it goes into the water, usually with an addled brain.

"Shaking hands" with the fish via the pole and dominating the fish as it swims hard and glides under the surface are the zenith of the experience. When a "hooked fish" wins the battle and swims away as the line snaps into midair, disappointment covers the face. The biggest ones get away; at least that is the common claim.

Of course size is a permanent curiosity. By the pull on the line and the "singing" of the pole as it bends, a fisherman conjures up visions of something huge and different from anything caught before. As the scales hit the top of the water, the vision is almost always diminished by reality. "He ain't as big as he pulled."

Lunch, al fresco in a boat in the middle of a lake, is five-star dining by any honest measure. Common eats such as sardines, Vienna sausage, spam, bologna, potted meat, saltine crackers, honey buns, soft drinks, and light bread suddenly become gourmet fare. The taste buds become more alive and acquire a new level of sensitivity. All is peace, fun and enjoyment save the ring that breaks off on the can of sausage, and the knife has to be pulled out to get at the tasty morsels inside.

The experience is not only the food but hugely the fellowship. Lunch is a good time to relax and share fishing stories, ever how made-up they may be, and life's experiences. Stories told and food eaten in God's restaurant takes on a special meaning and enjoyment.

We always ended the fishing trip with a "nice tired." Catching fish and enjoying life can take something out of you, but it always puts back in more than it takes, and that satisfaction makes it all worthwhile.

10

Hoyt's and Ozie's Store

Hoyt and Ozie Butler's Store

Standing at the corner of old US 84 and Highway 45 in Iron City, this old monument has weathered eighty, ninety, or more years, and today rests quietly with its walls retaining its vast memories. The walls cannot say a word, but if they could, they could recite a history of the town. Inside the store walls a business once thrived accompanied by a beehive of activity for the small community. The customers met and shared the experiences of humanity with Ozie, Hoyt, and their friends: grief, births, gossip, politics, hound dogs, disappointments, and successes.

I do not know of its construction date, but my first cousin and WWII veteran Dewey Mills has told me stories of going there as a teenager and getting a hamburger in the mid '30's. He described the hamburgers and Coke as being as good as it got. Ozie would cook hamburgers on an oil stove as they were ordered. Buying food ready-to-eat was a novelty since people habitually ate only at home.

Dewey stated that Hoyt and Ozie Butler ran the business in those days with a small lunch counter and a meat business. Alf Green remembered that Hoyt would barbecue meat in the ground adjacent to his store. He wrapped the meat in newspapers, placed it in a hole, and covered it with a layer of dirt and hot coals to cook overnight. The dirt insulated the newspapers from burning.

Roger Spooner described how Hoyt obtained his beef in the early days of his business. Hoyt had a financial arrangement with Henry Cummings who owned pasture land around Lela with grazing cattle. Hoyt would drive into the pasture, shoot a beef, and dress it right there in the field. He would haul the meat back to his store for further processing and storage in his icebox, cooled by ice. Wow! What a businessman, doing whatever it took to get the job done! Later he paid Cummings for the steer.

In the food production world of today, can we imagine how many people and costs were eliminated from the process? The steer did not get hauled to the stock yard, so they lost their cut. He incurred transportation costs, so no over-the-road hauling charges. No middle-man slaughter house, so the labor and packaging costs did not exist. No costs of transportation to the stores. No corporate ownership of stores getting their profit. Hoyt took it from the pasture to the cooler. He had to do that to make money. There is a lesson for business people of today, but they will have to figure it out.

In the early 1950s, the Butlers still ran the business, so under their management it survived twenty years or longer.

Late Saturday afternoons on the way back home from Donalsonville, Daddy and Mama would go by with me tagging along to purchase bologna, mullet, or oysters. It had evolved into a snack, meat, and seafood business plus the usual "grab-all" items of the day.

In those times people did not stop at a store only to shop. They counted on visiting with the owners and any customers that might be present, catching up on the news of the families and sharing fellowship. A quick trip into a store was an exception. With no phones of quantity, local news chiefly traveled person to person.

My memory is of Ozie being a sweet, small-framed, dark-haired lady with a ready smile. Somehow the years have taken away Hoyt's face and description. I do retain a fuzzy image of a portly gentleman.

During the early to mid '50s, the Butlers closed the place, leaving it sitting vacant for several years. The full service grocery stores in Donalsonville had taken their toll.

A Mr. Bainbridge (Bill Bainbridge's father) had a fishing bait and tackle business in the building circa 1960 for a year or so. Bill was one of my '63 classmates.

By the appearance of the rusting gasoline pumps and the tall shelter adjacent to it, someone had a service station and garage business there after I left the area.

With start-up businesses in Iron City being far between, this structure of heritage could have a long wait for the razing crew. Until then, the old block walls will continue to stand and hoard their sealed secrets.

11

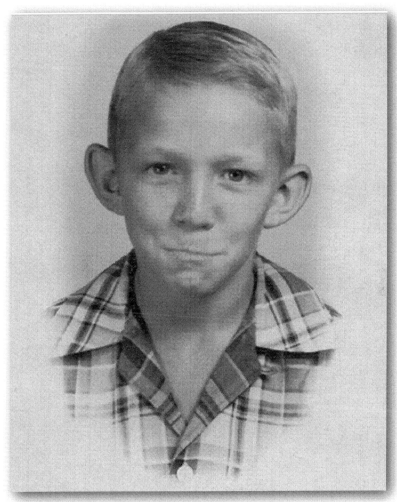

Samuel Baxley Mills (Fourth Grade)

Ugly Picture

This is a story I can tell only after old age has taken my judgment and shrunk my ego to the size of a politician's heart.

This picture shown below is a "one-of" school class picture taken in the fourth grade when in Miss Philmon's class. Sixty-one years ago the camera and subject came together to create the ugliest of works. Only a handful of people in my family have seen the picture for obvious reasons.

It took a lot of courage to take the pictorial disaster home to Loziane, but I suspected my psyche offered a subconscious method to such madness. She most assuredly expected an explanation of how I chose to frighten animals and small children on the fated day.

As possible with other children, I was born with a couple of problems: an underbite that no doubt caused my upper teeth to be crowded resulting in what was called in those days a "snaggle-toothed" appearance. My right incisor did not have enough space to come down in proper position, so it sat slightly higher than the other front teeth and pointed outward slightly. The front tooth next to it was crowded also, so it was pushed back out of line slightly. My smile did not look like everyone else's, so that was a problem, probably only to me but huge in my eyes. It became such a fixation in that year because the growth of my teeth had caused the abnormality to manifest itself fully in recent months.

Braces were not a financial possibility because of the huge cost of three hundred dollars. I had heard Mama mention the cost which had been incurred by at least two or three of my classmates' families. Three hundred dollars would be five thousand plus in today's dollars. That pile of money was not to be had by our family, and I well understood the impediment.

I told Mama I was trying to hide my teeth which had an unfortunate outcome for the picture. A simple no-teeth grin would have done the trick, but life did not work out that way. I could tell that she was disappointed and sad, and Lord knows maybe all of this was my simple way of crying out about what nature had done to me. Mama got a message for which she had no answer. She bought one 3x5 picture. My guess was it was her way of showing love in spite of the appearance of the picture.

When my other classmates were running around exchanging pictures, I was silent and told them that I did not have any.

Mama did not forget the experience. Eight years later she took me to Dr. Brooks in Colquitt who developed a cosmetic solution to the problem. He capped the incisor and extracted the tooth next to it. He put in a bridge that covered the space evenly, and I finally had a smile that I could share with others without being self-conscious. It was a happy day for me. It cost sixty-five dollars, but was worth a fortune in my eyes. Mama finally had her way and improved her son's smile and emotional well-being which she felt good about, too.

In 1978, through company insurance, I had the underbite corrected. A surgeon, Dr. Hardiston in Murfreesboro, TN, performed a jaw re-section in which he cut my bottom jaw in two on each side and pushed it back to create a normal bite. Having my jaws wired shut for five weeks taxed my mettle. Working at the time, I had to talk through my teeth, literally. Not being able to eat solid food, I took a blender on the road and ate blended soups and soft meals. What an unforgettable experience that was!

At last I had a normal smile and no longer had the pain in my jaws caused by an underbite.

God gave Mama a way to help me out and provided more reasons for me and her to be so thankful. Thank you, my Lord.

12

The Steyerman House

In late 2016 on the way to a doctor's appointment at Archbold in Thomasville, we were proceeding down Broad Street approaching our destination when out of the corner of my eye I saw a sign "The Steyerman House." Immediately my mind traced back to 1965 and how the domicile played a role in my life.

In 1904 a ritzy family, built the house, an elegant mansion of about 4700 square feet. The monied Steyerman family owned a department store and other interests in the city at the time.

In the spring of 1965, Sam was opening another short chapter of his life in Thomasville. His pal Buddy Odom had been working at Sunnyland Packing Company for an extended period since high school graduation.

Buddy was a member of the crack team of bacon slicers operating a bacon slicing machine cutting slabs into neat slices for packaging. It was a one-man machine. If you didn't like pig fat on your hands all day long, you did not apply. We did not notice the conspicuous absence of Muslims since neither Buddy nor I had heard of them.

In need of a short term job until I started to college in September, I asked Buddy to use his substantial clout to get me aboard the Sunnyland train. In short order he got me an interview with Russell Bozeman, the slave master in charge of the facility. With Buddy convincing Russell of what a hard worker and a pillar of the community I was, he put me to work with the understanding that I would leave and go to college in September.

Russell had a "dream job" working in the smoked meat department for me to become a "professional" ham hanger. God had decided to play a trick on me to see if I could figure out which was worse, ham hanging or picking cotton. He has quite a sense of humor. Handling wet, lardy hams all day and losing layer after layer of skin from my prune hands was not the job I had anticipated. Every day I reminded myself of why I needed to go to college and cotton picking remained the champion for worst job by a good margin.

Buddy was staying with his sister Martha and her husband Rex Hodges at the time. He and I wanted a bachelor pad, so we could have our own space and carouse at will. An ad in the newspaper caught our attention: room and bath for rent, twenty-five dollars per week. We decided to check it out for a match with our needs and our billfolds. Buddy was raking in $1.65 per hour, and I received a whopping $1.25 per hour. Time to live off the fat of the land. Yeah! Right! If Sunnyland had not provided a fringe benefit of cheap breakfast and lunch buffets for its workers, I may have learned to like the taste of tree bark and polk salad. We capped off each day with Chandler hamburgers, fries and a Coke, the ultimate in poor man's cuisine. We often wondered how the "worse off people" made it.

In 2016 when we were in Thomasville, I discovered the Chandler's building was still standing. A monument to "good eating" had survived all these years. Connie and I ate there, and I noticed it still carried the Chandler's name,34 but the food offering had changed substantially.

Visiting the Steyerman home, Buddy and I found Mae Steyerman to be a congenial, trusting senior that had a real deal to offer: a spacious, exquisitely furnished room with two beds, wardrobes, a tiled shower and an indoor toilet.

The house had those steam radiators along the walls as were in Donalsonville hospital when I was a kid. At the time it was the most spectacular house I had entered, so I marveled at the luxuries and the huge hall with hardwood floors that went from the kitchen to the front door. I wondered why if she were so rich, she could not let us stay for free to protect her since she lived alone. After thinking about it later, I decided maybe that is how she got rich. No freebies would come from her.

We enjoyed our stay in such a grand home. Our good buddy Terry Ingram came over and spent a day or two with us during his summer break from college. The stay could have been uneventful if Buddy had not surprised us one night. Standards of decency and a desire to shield the guilty will not allow me to divulge what happened, but it was a doozie. We three still laugh about the incident. All we have to do is ask Buddy, "What time is it?"

Being another reference of who I am, memories of the Steyerman House and Mae Steyerman with all the struggles of being young and foolish still linger so well. The past defines us and reveals volumes about ourselves.

13

Hitchhiking

Years ago when there was substantially more trust and love in this world, hitchhiking was commonplace. Locally a person on foot would wave at a coming car or pose with thumb turned up, and a ride usually assured in a few minutes.

My experience with hitchhiking relates to my brothers being in the army in the late '50s and early '60s. Several times I remember them hitchhiking home, and we would pick them up in Iron City. Once or twice through the courtesy of a veteran, they were lucky enough to get a ride all the way to our house,

Memories of WWII and the importance of our military were still fresh on people's minds. Tremendous respect for our soldiers motivated travelers who would readily stop for them. Military hitchhikers always wore the Army dress uniform, the key to a free ride, because it caught the attention of people driving and tapped into the huge respect for the military.

Oftentimes the owner of the vehicle had served in WWII and understood very well the need to help out a fellow comrade in arms.

My brothers Lloyd and Jerome wanted to be dropped at Newton, Georgia to catch a ride. Mama, Daddy and I would drive them to the intersection of the Colquitt-Newton Road and the highway north to Albany. We would wait until they caught a ride which was usually a few minutes, and they would wave back to us as they boarded a car. A compromising situation with a traveler never happened.

Since those days, the world has become a lot less trusting. Two fears come with hitchhiking: Will the driver of the car harm the rider? Will the hitchhiker harm the driver? Stories in the news tell us the last acts of unfortunate people can be associated with hitchhiking.

Those safer, simpler days continue to be a model example in many ways. We recognize the progress our country has made, but in a few areas it is obvious we have taken steps backward; that's life.

14

Pound Cake

A couple years ago Ina Trawick Fowler related a story regarding Mama's pound cakes. Ina stated that Mama entered a pound cake in a competition in which she won first place because in Ina's opinion she mixed her batter by hand. I am not sure of the alternatives in those days, but a mechanized tool could have been used per preference. A hand-held manual beater comes to mind as a possibility.

Yes, Mama mixed all her pound cakes by hand. I still preserve a poignant memory of her with cake batter on both hands massaging the batter in a large, deep bowl. It took considerable time to mix it thoroughly, as I watched the minutes drag being ready to lick the bowl. Amazingly salmonella did not come calling from the raw eggs.

The plain butter pound cake proved to be Mama's best offering. The buttery goodness with a glass of milk was among the premium food delights of those days. Occasionally, Daddy and I would leave the field and go to the house for cake and milk in mid-afternoon. Expanding waistlines with our workload had no concern for us. By working so hard, the calories were readily burned, and our bodies starved for more.

Daddy always liked something sweet on the table: syrup, jelly or preserves for breakfast, pound cake or another dessert such as egg custard or rice pudding for the other two meals.

Other than the delicious taste, another reality caused pound cakes to be served so often. The butter, milk and eggs we produced on the farm, so no outflow of cash. Egg custards were popular for a similar reason.

When Mama made rice, she prepared enough extra to make rice pudding, a cheap but delicious dessert. The careful use of finances and assets was inherent in her thinking.

Recently I have begun baking desserts. So far pecan pie, banana bread and pecan chewies have been mastered. Soon I plan to tackle a pound cake. I keep putting it off because it surely will not be as good as hers, but the time is nigh to take a shot at it. Whatever I make will be scrumptious—with a glass full of memories.

15

Roger and Eloise Spooner

Roger Spooner, in His Words

Oct 27, 1941, Roger joined the Navy. When I asked, "Why the Navy?" he replied, "I did not want the Army and I wanted to get away from the farm. I was tired of following that mule."

"It was a six year enlistment." He pointed at a newspaper picture in the room from Albany showing a group of enlistees he joined who traveled on to Macon where they were sworn in. He went from Macon to Norfolk, Virginia, for a three month boot camp.

His plans to come home in December for Christmas were interrupted when the Japs bombed Pearl Harbor on the seventh of the month. With the Yorktown being in dry dock in Norfolk, the ship became his assignment, and they passed through the Panama Canal on Christmas Day headed for the Pacific theater. The ship, being an aircraft carrier, bombed Jap positions in the Marshall and Gilbert Islands before docking at Pearl Harbor.

At Pearl Harbor they took on a crew of pilots and airplanes and the ship headed for the Coral Islands. The crew did not know where they were going for security reasons.

Roger mentioned the censorship of all their mail. They turned over their letters for home unsealed for screening of any information regarding their positions. Any information of this nature was blacked out so it could not be read.

He joked "pineapple" meant Pearl Harbor and "kangaroo" meant Australia, so those words were always blacked out. His parents could make nothing of one of the last letters he wrote before the end of the war because a large number of words were covered in black.

The ship headed for an area near the cost of Australia where they had the Coral Sea battle on May 8. The Yorktown was bombed and torpedoed in the battle, but another ship, the Lexington, was sunk.

The Yorktown made it back to Pearl Harbor the latter part of May and dry docked for seventy-two hours. With damage to the ship, the crew assumed they were going back to the states, but they were unaware Japs were trying to take Midway at the time.

When Roger woke the next morning, he went to the stern of the ship and saw the sun. Upon seeing this, he stated "I knew darn well we were not headed to the states. We were headed toward Japan."

In the next day or two, the military broke the Japanese code, so the command knew what the Japanese were planning. The Japs were coming to meet the Yorktown and were trying to locate it. The enemy had a big fleet, but the Yorktown sank four of their ships in the battle.

Roger, a first loader on a five inch gun with his shells weighing fifty-four pounds, was in the fourth division on the Yorktown

The next morning the skipper told the crew that the Jap military code had been broken revealing the enemy wanted to take Midway, about fifteen hundred miles from Pearl Harbor. The Yorktown went to meet the enemy, and Roger noted, "That's where we tangled up with them." No other aircraft carrier was attacked on the US side.

"They were out to get us. They would fly over cruisers, battleships and destroyers leaving them untouched and came for us."

The dive bombers came right out of the sun and bombed the ship while the torpedo planes came right on the water. There were dozens of the planes. The attack came in the morning, so by 1:00 p.m. their skipper informed them that the ship had lost all power. "We were dead in the water and sinking."

Roger abandoned ship at 1:00 p.m. wearing only his skivvies and a life jacket. With twenty-five hundred crew on the ship, "We had an ocean full of people floating around out there." Luckily he was rescued the next morning.

I asked him what he thought about during the night. Roger replied, "There a no words to express what went on in my mind." When I asked about family, he said," Yes sir, I thought about family and thought of Iron City. I thought I would never see it again."

When Roger returned to Pearl Harbor, he learned that two hundred ninety-two enlisted men were lost and ninety-three officers, mostly pilots who were shot down.

On Pearl Harbor they took the survivors to a Marine base where they had no clothes and had to sleep on the ground. The next morning when they picked them up, the skipper told the marines to open their lockers for the men to get some clothes.

He said they were filthy, dirty from oil that was three to four inches deep on the side of the ship on which they went overboard. Since it was a crude, heavy oil, it became impossible to recognize each other. "You could not wash it off. You had to wear it off."

They placed the survivors in Camp Andrew which was out in the woods where they had tents and cots to sleep on. The crew remained encamped for two months and could not write a letter home. They had no paper to write on. Per Roger, "We had nothing."

At that time his folks back home did not know because nothing had been reported by the military. "They still had not reported the loss of the Lexington in the Coral Sea. With the Yorktown sunk, the military command did not want to report either as sunk for morale reasons. They kept our crew silent."

For about four months Roger's folks thought he was missing until they were told he survived.

Roger went to Admiral Nimitz's headquarters at Pearl Harbor, known as CENPAC, which was at the oil docks in Pearl Harbor, in June and stayed there until February of the next year. "I was driving for a one star Admiral. All I had to do was wash the car up, keep it clean and drive him anywhere he wanted to go."

One morning Roger was headed to the officers' quarters to pick up the Admiral, and a Marine officer waved him down who had been standing at a bus shelter. "I wasn't fully dressed, not all squared up nor had my stars formed." The Admiral Nimitz told him to settle down and take him to his office. "That's as close as I ever got to Nimitz, sitting in the seat with him."

Note:
Admiral Nimitz played a major role in WWII as Commander In Chief United States Pacific Fleet, for US naval forces and Commander in Chief, Pacific Ocean Areas, for US and Allied air, land, and sea.

The USS NIMITZ is the first ship in the NIMITZ - class of nuclear-powered aircraft carriers and the first ship in the Navy named after Fleet Admiral Nimitz.

Staying at the assignment until February of '43, Roger told the Admiral whom he chauffeured that he had to go home. He stated, "I have not been home since I joined and I have got to go."

The Admiral replied, "I can get you home, but I can't get you back." This meant that Roger would lose his good duty assignment. The Admiral indicated, "You will have to take 'new construction' when your leave is over."

"I had been considering submarine duty because the pay was good. It was half again larger than my current pay. It was like flight pay."

Taking submarine duty, he was told to report to a base in New London, Connecticut after his leave.

He spent six days of his thirty-day leave traveling by train from California to Iron City.

"Back in those days we had no cushions to sit on. We had old wooden benches. I was worn to a frazzle. I slept on the floor. That was the only carpet they had, so I slept on the floor. They had bathrooms on the train, but there was not much to them. They were 'get-by.'"

Roger made it home where he married his first wife.

Traveling two days by train to New London, he received submarine training and went to diesel school. He then caught a train back to California. "I did not know what was going to happen. The first thing I knew, they sent me to Perth, Australia."

At Perth he went aboard the USS Jag 259 on which he went on nine war patrols. With long assignments, they patrolled for sixty to ninety days and commonly fired the bulk of their torpedoes. The Jag once sank five ships in one night.

The war was slowing down, and unknowingly the submarine docked at an island where his brother Luther who was in the army came through a few days later. They did not know this until after the war.

About this time in the summer of '45, atom bombs had been dropped on Hiroshima and Nagasaki, resulting in the Japanese preparing to surrender.

Roger next went to Yokosuka, Japan. Being a Jap sub base, there were a large number of two-man subs. Roger and his fellow crew members took the subs out into the harbor and sank them.

The crew noticed a lot of activity in the harbor and saw a number of ships and a battleship. "There was no communication in those days. You did not learn anything." Later they learned that the Japanese were signing the peace treaty with MacArthur.

On November 1, 1945, Roger headed back to the states and moved through the Panama Canal on December 1 headed for Norfolk, Virginia, where Roger received leave for a trip home.

"I was married about two and one-half years and had seen my wife less than thirty days. We had gotten a divorce by that time, but I didn't know it. I had sent Mother and Daddy up to Columbus to find out who had been sleeping in my bed." They found trouble, so the marriage was over.

He never saw her again after returning home.

After the war, Roger lucked into eighteen months of easy duty at Key West.

"That's where I about got killed in a motorcycle wreck. They said they thought I was going to Cuba. I ran off the end of a boulevard down there about drunk. I spent several months in the hospital and about died." Today his left arm will not rise above his shoulder.

A guy was riding behind Roger named Tige. "I lost him at eighty-five mph when I hit the brakes. We were both drunk. We had been up to a little place called Weaver near Boka Chika."

I told Roger that I had not known of the wild side of him. He stated, "After four years of service, I had pretty well got adapted to all the bars."

He once made an overnight ride from Key West to Iron City on the motorcycle, not a small feat.

Roger is infamous for burning down a gas station in Tallahassee including the owners's domicile. In the era it was common for a proprietor's home to be built above the gas pumps.

Roger stopped at the station on his way back to Key West. Aware that the air breather on the motorcycle had fallen off back down the road and was lost in the dark, he cautioned the guy to not get gas on the very hot area. The owner spilled some gas unknowingly. "When I fired it off, it lit up the station's gas tank."

Roger ran and looked back as the tanks, house, and motorcycle went up in flames. Catching a cab which took him to the local airbase, he caught a military plane to Key West.

He told an unusual story of being broke roughly fifty to seventy-five miles north of Miami. Wearing his uniform, he walked in a local bank to get some help. "I told this guy I got to have some money. I'm headed home."

When the banker started asking a lot of questions, Roger asked him to call the Merchants and Farmers bank in Donalsonville, tell them who he was and that he needed some money. The man talked to Henry Cummings. "Doggone it. I got my money right there. I got money on a man's word. You try it today," he declared, laughing.

Asking Roger when his mother and daddy were married: "That's a good question." Not knowing, I told him that I would look it up.

When Luke, born October 4, 1883, and Delia, born June 4, 1891, started out their marriage, they lived on land Peter Cummings owned near Lake Seminole. At the time Roger's granddaddy Joe Spooner and Peter Cummings owned huge acreage in the county, so Peter wanted Luke to farm a tract on River Road south of Charles Childree's land today. They lived there less than a year after being married January 3, 1909, in Lela, and moved back to the old home place, Joe Spooner's house, circa summer of 1909. Luke and Delia lived with Joe Spooner until Joe built a new house down the road. Their first child Eron was born September 20, 1909. Roger and all of his brothers and sisters were born and reared in the old Joe Spooner home.

Joe Spooner's wife Mary Jane Lane Spooner died December 2, 1914. Roger stated that she passed away in Spooner Field, the location of their second home near today's Lake Seminole. He said they were together at the home, but Joe went back to their primary domicile near Lela that day. A black man with her got word to Joe of her passing. Roger indicated that it was most of a days ride between the two homes by horse and buggy.

Joe built another house up the road circa 1916 for his new wife where in the future Bud Youmans and Lila Mae Spooner Youmans lived and raised their children. Margaret Gainey from Cairo and Joe were married and had one child, Lila Mae in 1919.

Roger said that Margaret's twin sister came to live with them. "He got two women at one time."

Roger explained something that I had always wondered about. When Luke, Daddy, and I would be fishing on Lake Seminole, he would talk about grazing cattle in an area he would point to which was then covered by water. Asking Roger how Luke got land down at the lake, he responded, "The land belonged to Henry Cummings, and Luke was getting free grazing. He had a bunch of cows. I helped take them down there. He would go down about every day to check on them."

I asked Roger whether children were born at home or in the hospital. They were born at home where doctors would make house calls on horse and buggy. Roger remembered that Dr. John I. Spooner delivered him and gave him his middle name, "Hern." Delia had told Roger that Dr. Spooner had a friend in college named Hern.

Roger said Dr. Spooner owned a large piece of land the other side of Jakin which he sold back to the government. He recalled that the Federal Government would build a small house on sixty-two acres and give it to someone in need to farm. Dr. Spooner accumulated tracts of that land near Howard's Mill.

Wondering about tenant farmers, I asked Roger if Luke had any tenants. Roger said two families of colored people lived on the farm and described the relationship as follows: "We worked arm and hand with them. Sometimes we ate at their house, and they would eat at our house. There have been some helluva changes since back in them days."

A farm size was roughly measured by how many mules a farmer had. They had twelve to fifteen mules and had a couple of riding cultivators which were pulled by two mules. He said, "You would sit there and guide the wheels with foot pedals, control your depth and everything. It was a lot easier than stepping over mule hockey."

The family made cane syrup for their use and to sell commercially. "Daddy would put it in fifty-five gallon barrels. They would haul it to customers on a wagon." As for the potential use of the syrup in moonshining, Roger indicated, "The law would follow that syrup."

"In the winter we would kill and dress eighteen or twenty hogs. People we knew would come from miles around to help. They would take home two or three of the hogs."

"We would put the hogs in a kettle of hot water and add a little turpentine to it, so we could pull the hair off. Controlling the temperature was critical or the meat would be burned."

"We milked maybe six head of cows morning and night. It took a lot of milk and butter for the family. I could handle the clabber by mixing some syrup with it but could not develop a taste for the buttermilk."

The first vehicle he could remember his daddy owning was about a 1936 second hand Ford pickup. He said, "A tank of gas would last a long time because he did not drive it much. We usually rode to town on a mule and wagon."

"Some of us was going home from town after dark with no lights on the wagon. A man named Zuback ran into us on an old log cart about 11 o'clock. I don't know what kind of truck it was, but we were right about where the airport is today. It knocked the wagon, mules and us right into the fence."

"He was not going very fast because it was a bumpy dirty road. He knocked the body of the wagon up on the mules' backs, and the mules stood there frozen, scared to death."

"Me, Luther, Joe and James Sauls were in the wagon. Miriam Minter who was dating a girl down that way came by and helped us."

Roger remembered the crowded streets in Donalsonville. "My old car would run hot looking for a parking place."

When asked about going to church on Sunday, he replied, "You darn right we did. The family went to the Baptist church in Donalsonville every Sunday on the wagon. It took a couple hours to get there. The preacher would go home with you. He was hunting a good meal."

The Luke Spooner family had a long history with the Baptist church. Roger said the one they attended is still standing on Tennile Avenue. It is the old stucco building, currently used as a Masonic lodge, across the street from the present Baptist church. When he was a young boy, Roger joined the church. He stated, "I am now the oldest member of the church."

I asked Roger whether he and Eloise had a church wedding. He laughed, "Hah! Let me tell you about that wedding. Back in those days you could not buy any gas unless somebody was hooked up to get it for you. We went by Mama and Daddy's house to tell them we were going to get married. Eloise's step daddy was Jake Lane. Her daddy was killed by a power line when she was two or three years old."

"We stopped by and Daddy had a long conversation with Eloise because I had already had one marriage that did not stick. He told her what she could look out for, what she had better do and all this. I had done been through one marriage which did not mean much to me because I was overseas all that time."

"The car had no headlights because they were out. That was right after the war. People were not able to buy a lot of things."

"We went to Bainbridge and did not know what was coming over the fence. We went in that court house, headed down a hall and had no idea where the Ordinary's office was. We didn't even have a marriage license. It was getting late in the evening, and the lady was locking the door. I said, 'hold on don't lock that door yet.' We came here to get married. We are here on a car without headlights, and we have to find a place to stay. I am not going to sleep in the back seat and her in the front seat on our wedding night. We would not be married." I did not touch her until we were married.

"She turned around and went back in there and said, "Who's your witness?" I said, My God, I have not needed a witness all my life. I stepped out there on the street and saw a man walking by. I said, I'll pay you five dollars to be a witness."

Jokingly I reminded Roger that he paid me five dollars a day to drive his tractor around 1965 so I got gipped. Roger laughed out loud.

Asked about Spooner family reunions, he did not remember any. "We had a big family, and we had people living in the Spooner house with us: Aunt Anna, her husband James and their children, Eugene and Helene. We had a house full of people."

When I asked how many rooms were in the old Spooner house he said, "There was four bedrooms downstairs and two upstairs, but they did not use the upstairs much."

I asked Roger if the home had flush toilets. "No, they were outside. No toilets were put in until after I left home for the service. Daddy had one put in next to their bedroom."

Did they have one for the females and one for the males? "We had a three-holer, and we all used the same one. And on top of that we had the Sears and Roebuck catalog."

Did he play sports in high school? "No, when you got home, you had a job. I went to Lela school for several years. After Lela, I went to Donalsonville."

"Peter Cummings owned Lela but not the school. He gave Lela his wife's name in her honor. The school was upstairs in a big building. About three-fourths of it has been taken down, but the rest of it is still there."

"Mother and Daddy married in Lela and left in a buggy headed to the Peter Cummings place on the river where they lived the first year."

"Lela used to have logging. Peter brought timber in on a railroad to his lumber mill. Peter's land holdings in the area grew to as large as 75,000 acres to supply trees to the mill. I have been in the commissary that was there. Whenever you worked for Peter, he paid you with a chip. You turned around and bought your groceries at the commissary, and he got that chip right back. You would get the chip again next week."

"The railroad ran all the way down to the lower end of the county."

"I remember a teacher Mrs. Wood who lived in a house where Lila Mae was at. Miss Maggie had a colored driver named Noah Thomas who would haul the teacher back and forth to Lela."

"The teacher taught all of us. There would be three grades in one doggone room. When you were having your class, they were over there studying for the next class. You paid attention after you got your "hiney" tore up. You had better not let it be known at home that you got a whipping."

Which of your parents did the discipline? "Whichever one was handy. If you teed 'em off, you were in trouble."

How did he get into the trucking business? "In 1954 a guy was in the trucking business and he got out. I had seen his truck, so I said I'd buy his truck and hook up with the same outfit. It was John Cummings, Jr. He didn't "make a go of it," so I decided I would try it."

"He leased with Watkins Motor Lines out of Thomasville, Georgia. I went over there, saw Bill Watkins and signed up. I stayed with him a year and a half. I pulled a refrigerated trailer all the way up into Minnesota and back down to Miami. You had to have a helper driver. You would crawl back into the sleeper and go to bed hoping he wouldn't hit anybody and kill you."

"I once got back to Montgomery and was disgusted. I had a load of concentrated orange juice and was headed somewhere up north. We did not have air conditioning and it was hot. I called Bill and told him I had filled up the Therma King. I told him that if he did not want to send me a dime to clean up what was owed me that would be all right. I am fed up. I have got a belly full and am going back to the house. I left his trailer. I was pulling his trailer with my tractor."

"I went back home and got into short hauling and farming. I hauled for anybody that needed hauling."

How did he handle trucking and farming? "Rudolph Shores farmed with me. Rudolph was a good man. Everybody had two jobs."

"I bought the home place in 1974, three hundred seventy-eight acres. I was running a bulldozer for hire, too. I had two bulldozers and a John Deere 544 front end loader with four wheel drive and cleared a bunch of land for people. I was running the bulldozers for $12.50 per hour. That was good money in them days. I did whatever it took to make a dollar. I had a good woman behind me, and I miss her."

"I have been blessed. God has been good to me. I will be ninety-five years old come November 18. I came in yesterday on my eighteen wheeler—the oldest truck driver on the road."

"The DOT man says, "Who hires you?" I told him nobody hires me. I don't even draw a check (laughing)" He said, "You're ninety-four years old. Have you thought about retiring?" I told him, "Now that you have brought it up. I haven't."

"I've had accidents. I had dropped my telephone and I was trying to pick it up. I was running along about sixty-five miles an hour trying to get it, and the first thing I know I was in the ditch. I was pulling a dump trailer hauling lime from Arlington to Bainbridge. I rolled it over on the rider's side and skidded down that highway and dumped the whole load of lime."

"Another time I remember Mama was sick, and I was trying to pick up a pack of chewing gum on the floor. The first thing I knew I was in the ditch, and I looked up and saw a driveway going to a man's house. The driveway was about belt high. I had my cruise set on fifty-eight miles per hour. I had put on my brakes, but I hit that driveway with an empty trailer behind. The troopers said tractor and trailer were in the air for forty-one feet. I went back across the road and missed a light pole by about a foot and stopped. I was able to drive it back home without much damage."

"The first thing I knew a man's wife was opening the door on the passenger side, standing in mud and her husband was right behind her on his phone."

The closest Roger came to dying was circa 2003 when he drove to his house to swap trailers. Eloise, not knowing anything about driving a tractor, saved his life that day.

"I did not set the air brakes on the tractor and while I was unhooking it, the tractor rolled back pinning me between the tractor and trailer."

"There she was not knowing anything."

Eloise was able to get in the tractor, figure out the gears and move it so she could get Roger free. God took charge.

"I blacked out. I stayed in Dothan six days and nights. They thought I would not make it. I was nearly dead."

Roger joined Connie and me for lunch at Jo's restaurant where we informally continued our conversation. Roger spoke of the importance of Eloise in his life. He goes at least once every day to her grave and sits in a chair. Sixty-nine years of marriage has created quite a bond which cannot be replaced.

He cautioned me to love Connie while I can because I will surely miss her. Those are truthful words that I have heeded well.

Roger has been unusually blessed throughout his life. Coming from a fine old family with deep roots, having a faithful, loving wife and five loving boys who had their moments tempting fate, he has enjoyed life's blessings. Between the War, the motorcycle wreck, the service station burning and the tractor accidents, he must have kept the Good Lord busy watching over him, perhaps because He had a high purpose for Roger.

16

Atwood Lane, Nonagenarian

In 2015 Connie and I had the pleasure of visiting ninety-four-years-old Atwood Lane in Room 109 at the Seminole Manor Nursing Home. What a great visit it was! He rattled on many subjects and we listened, trying to hang onto every word. His stories of old riveted our attention. Effortlessly he reeled off names and dates from long ago as if it were yesterday—a very sharp mind for anyone at any age.

His parents were Will and Ellen Cross Lane who raised their children on four hundred acres of land off HWY 45 near the Burl Lane Road and north of Iron City. His brothers Jack and Bennie have passed on, but he has a sister Martha Ann "Huck" Lane McDaniel, who lives today north of Iron City off the Colquitt Road. Another sister Lucy, age 93, was married to Plug Hornsby and was also a current resident of Seminole Manor. A sister Jewell Powell lived in south Florida but has passed.

Martha Ann has the uncommon nickname of Huck from being called Huckleberry in her childhood. I had not met Huck until Betty Ausley passed away in 2014. Huck, a distinctive personality, honest and without euphemisms, was a delight in conversation. I laughed hard at her story of being left at her sister's house in south Florida by her brother Bennie.

Learning that she liked fish, I took her a huge mess of crappie filets a few weeks after our first meeting.

In 1951 Atwood married Mae Herring who had two boys from a previous marriage. She was originally from South Carolina but was living in Bainbridge when they met.

Atwood did not remember the details of how he started playing stringed instruments. He was twelve when he started playing the guitar, a Stella make. Later in his teen years, he mastered the mandolin playing one with a banjo uke. He enjoyed playing the mandolin accompanied by Mack Cross and Howard "Speedy" Lane on guitars.

Atwood's love of country music and his affiliation with my first cousin Dewey Mills, who lived in Cairo, Georgia at the same time as he, were my connections to this old country music fan. He said after he started playing, he was so skilled that people would come pick him up to play at square dances in the area. He grew up loving the music of Bob Wills who was known as the King of Western Swing, a legend in the '40s and '50s with his songs being constantly played on the radio.

Those old enough to remember Johnny Mack Brown western movies will appreciate that he came from Dothan, Alabama and was a star football player at the University of Alabama. Atwood remembered that Brown came every year to the Dothan Peanut Festival. A few Johnny Mack Brown movies rounded out the western motif at the Dunn Theater in the '50s.

Four or five years back I invited Atwood and Dewey, both WWII veterans, to eat fish at our weekend house on Lake Seminole. We had a great visit, and they enjoyed the fish. To me those guys were royalty, and I felt lucky to be in their presence.

Atwood served in WWII, but in his words, "I never had to leave Texas." He said he served one year at San Antonio and three years at Gainesville, TX. Laughingly, he said a few guys had to stay back here to keep the ladies company. He was not speaking of only sharing moony eyes knowing Atwood's fun nature.

After the War, Atwood hooked up with local country music players: my daddy Sam Mills, Dixie Maude Williams Jones, LJ King and Sampson Waddell. Depending on who was available to attend, the group of instrumentalists played at square dances in people's homes. Their performances entertained the country folks and was eagerly anticipated and appreciated by the dancers. Atwood stated that Anderson Williams' house was the most frequent place they performed.

During the late '20s or '30s, he indicated that my daddy played piano at a dance hall which was located across the street from Emmett Ward's store and approximately where the Iron City fire department is currently located. Daddy had given up playing the piano, which he played by ear, by the time I came along. His talent was the mandolin and guitar when I attended get-togethers in the '50s and '60s.

A husband of his wife's friend helped Atwood secure a job in the printing business. He spent fifty years plus maintaining the equipment and printing at two newspapers in Cairo. Atwood witnessed quite an evolution in the printing business during his career all the way from handset type to ink jet printers.

By doing his job and getting the papers out, Atwood joked that he helped Marvin Griffin become governor. Marvin, a popular governor from Bainbridge in the '50s, lost a fourteen year old daughter Patricia Ann in Atlanta's Winecoff hotel fire on December 7, 1946, per Atwood. At the time it was the deadliest hotel fire in US history.

Born in 1921, Atwood had witnessed many trying times and events. He spoke of the Depression, the two-wheel Hoover carts pulled by horses or mules, the shortage of money, and running Model T's on kerosene. Since they had a sizable farm, his family ate well during this period by growing their own food and livestock.

Two-wheel Hoover carts were a new term for me. Researching on the internet, I learned that these carts were a form of transportation during the Depression and were built by taking the rear axle and wheels off a car and attaching them to a cart. The cart was pulled by either a mule or horse. The drivers of these carts would stop at service stations for water for the horse or mule and air for the tires for which there was no charge. Yielding a softer ride and making the carts easier to pull versus buggy wheels, the vehicles enjoyed popularity among the hard pressed of the era.

Atwood said that one of my great uncle Carl Spooner's daughters, Mary Virginia, was born in 1923, and he became good friends with her. Recalling they dated a few times, he stated she had the most beautiful blue eyes he had seen. He knew all of Uncle Carl's children, Mary, Sybil, Louise, Euna and Don.

Atwood related a humorous story from about five years back. My first cousin Dewey and Atwood were invited to Steinhatchee, Florida to a restaurant run by my first cousin Herbert Mills' (WWII vet) girl friend. Herbert was about eighty-eight or eighty-nine at the time, so his having a girl friend should bring much credit to him for his male prowess.

Dewey and Atwood understood that they were going there to eat seafood for which they had their appetites well whetted. Upon arriving, they learned that only fried chicken was served. They laughed and had poultry for lunch though Atwood and Dewey had to hide their extreme disappointment.

What a wonderful visit we had with Atwood! His ninety-four years had brought a wealth of experiences worth hearing. He is one of the last of what has been called "The Greatest Generation," tough people of the WWII era who preserved our way of life.

As we were getting ready to leave, Atwood said that he had to say something that could make me mad. I told him not to worry since getting angry at him would be hard to do. He said that I could leave Connie with him because he was taken by her beauty. We all laughed. I told him that would not be possible since she and I are a team, impossible to pull apart—but "nice try."

17

Feed Mills

Today Roadside Milling, an old memory, stands idle waiting for eventual demolition. In the late '50s and early '60s, feed processing played an important roles as a key component of the livestock business in Seminole County; it thrived for approximately ten or fifteen years.

Only three feed mills existed in Seminole County in the period: Roadside Milling, Earl Gibbons' mill in Donalsonville and Raymond Mathis' mill in Iron City. During their existence, Daddy did business with all three. I remember going fishing once or twice with Earl, his son Ward, and Daddy, a good friend of Earl's, on Lake Seminole via Desser Landing.

Roadside remains as the most intact of the facilities. Iron City Milling still has a portion of its grain storage silos with the mill, front office and sales area having been demolished. The Earl Gibbons mill, near Five Points across the railroad tracks in the edge of Barber Town, has disappeared.

Mathis sold shotgun shells, so he got feed-crushing and ammunition business from us. I always liked the warmth of the main office in the winter time, a good place to knock off the chill. The two Mathis sons, Darryl and Howell, worked with their daddy.

My strongest memory is of Roadside Milling because both of my brothers worked there circa 1957-59. Bartow Gibson owned the business with Bud Youmans managing the operation and WH Miller working in a supervisory role. Located on HWY 39 about a mile south of the intersection with GA 285, it drew a steady stream of farmers needing corn or other grains crushed and mixed with supplements.

The business had a social aspect; farmers would see each other and catch up on what was going on in their lives while their grain was being processed. The waiting queue always had at least a customer or two in line for processing.

As I look at that Roadside picture, I can hear the whining sound of the mill and imagine the thousands of bags of feed that went through it and onto waiting trucks for transport to the farms in the area.

Lloyd bagged and sewed a large number of crocus bags of feed during his employment. After the bag attached to the feed chute was full, customers would see him or another worker quickly pierce the top of the bag eight or ten times across its top width with a large hand-held needle and twine and tie it off. The bags would be placed near the load-out door for stacking onto the truck when the batch was complete.

Accidentally contributing a piece of his little finger to the milling operation while working with a high speed V-belt doing maintenance, his little finger, covered by a glove, made contact with the belt. Lloyd lost about a quarter inch off the finger as the belt cut through the glove and flesh.

To feed our pigs Daddy would have me load a few bushels of corn out of our crib into the back of our pickup for processing into feed at the mill. He would always have them grind the shucks separately and add molasses for the milk cow to eat. It was not exactly a great source of nutrition, but the cow liked the sweet molasses.

Roadside had the only mobile feed mill in the county which was operated by my brother Jerome and a black gentleman named Pap. They would go to a farm, crush the corn or other grain right out of the storage bin, and bag it.

Jerome and Pap were always trying to show each other how strong they were. Pap was a well-built fellow with arms the size of men's necks, probably a thirty inch waist, and about five foot seven. Jerome was as fit as he would ever be. Lloyd told me that a man got cross with Jerome at Estes night club one night, and Jerome body slammed him. Fight over!

As part of the operation, they would deliver feed to farms when ordered. One afternoon about five o'clock, Lloyd stopped by our house with a load of chicken feed. He asked if I wanted to ride with him near

Bainbridge to a lady name Cassie Eagleton's house to make a delivery. She was a chicken producer of size for the day. After we backed up to her barn, I understood why he invited me. At the ripe young age of about twelve, I helped him unload the truck with sweat dripping in the summer heat.

Lloyd and Jerome together bought a red and white 1958 Ford Fairlane for the paltry sum of $2,000 compared to todays prices while working at Roadside. To my young eyes it was the most beautiful vehicle I had seen. Forever they struggled with the problem of whose turn it was to use it and how to make the payments when each of them made only about $40-$50 per week. Of course car payments were a lot smaller in that time. The army drafted Lloyd in 1959 or 1960 and Jerome volunteered around the same time. I don't know what happened to the beautiful car. They may have gotten someone to take up payments on it.

Exactly when Roadside Milling closed is unknown to me. I am fairly sure it was still in operation in 1963 when I finished high school. At a point in the mid to late '60s, Roadside was to be no more. Bartow built another feed mill adjacent to the railroad tracks on the east side of Donalsonville endeavoring to take advantage of rail transportation. It did not last for very many years. The structure which has housed a few businesses over the years remains intact, and a business operates out of it now.

Gone are the days of hometown feed mills. The economics of volume dictated that livestock feed had to be produced by large mills and in quantity. Flint River Mills (FRM) of Bainbridge operated back in my teen years and still functions today as a viable business, a survivor.

Small feed mills were an important part of the local economy for a limited period of time. As with most innovations, they came, they served a useful purpose, and they disappeared as a better, more efficient way of grinding and distributing feed was developed.

18

A Visit With Clifford

September 10, 2015, Connie and I stopped by to see Mrs. Clifford Cannington, soon to be ninety-two, and had a delightful visit. Mrs. Cannington's warm, friendly manner made us feel so much at home and welcome. It was as if we had known her intimately our whole lives.

Being still nimble and energetic, she gushed with information of times long passed. We digested every word she spoke because she had lived those long ago days and knew the subjects well.

Mrs. Hagan, wife of the Hagan's Turpentine Still owner, had sold the property Clifford's house rests on to her daddy. Clifford noted the presence of a "log bar" in that era across the road in front of their house which pulled in the local tipplers.

Clifford had several anecdotes from long ago. She related that a few couples including her and her husband used to go to the Spooner springs for fish suppers. On one occasion Brandy Trawick had sampled the mash and started cutting up as he could do. All of a sudden the power went out, and they were in darkness. In a few minutes Brandy slammed his fist on a table and exclaimed, "Let there be light!" and the power immediately returned. They all had a good laugh and wondered of his connection with the Man Upstairs.

She recalled having lunch with Luke and Delia Spooner, when Luke told her that she could get all the food on her plate she wanted, but she had better eat it all. Clifford said she felt a lot of pressure. Food was truly held in high reverence in those days, but surely my great uncle was joshing with her.

Remembering Betty Ausley, Clifford stated that Betty was always trying to pull a joke on someone. Once she loaded up a dish Slim was going to eat with hot sauce, much to his dismay. Sounds like the Betty we all knew.

When the REA was getting started in the county, Clifford stated that Luke Spooner came to her daddy and told him that he could invest in the startup for fifty dollars. Luke said that he was putting in that amount. Her daddy had to sell a cow to raise enough money and bought a share in the REA. The rural families received electricity, and the few who bought shares had invested wisely. Clifford said that a few years back the value of the fifty dollar share was over $2,000, a great investment.

Others may know the answer to the following trivia question but I did not: What was Police Chief Cannington's first name? He was the father of Clifford's husband and helped many of us cross the street safely at the corner where Goree Johnson's store resided. His name was Leanza.

Clifford showed us pictures of her children, her grandchildren and great grandchildren of which we could tell she is so proud. She also presented an article from the Donalsonville News highlighting her highest point total at bridge play with other seniors. She is remarkably sharp for someone of her age and could cause many younger people to be envious of her clarity.

Clifford is such a treasure and has been so blessed to have a long, meaningful, happy life. God bless her. We are looking forward to stopping by to see her again or maybe having lunch with her and Kaye in Donalsonville.

19

Down-Home Fun

When checking the definition of down-home, I found: "connected with an unpretentious way of life, especially that of rural peoples or areas," a very accurate description of people and the way of life in the 1950s. Not many Seminole Countians had enough material possessions to be considered pretentious. The overly pretentious may have received a one way trip to Chattahoochee. The "financial playing field" of the day was a lot more level than it is today and down-home activities were plentiful.

The populace worked hard but lacked the many amusements of today for relaxation and entertainment. Beyond the radio which was found in all households and maybe an occasional "picture show," get-togethers in the evenings were a prime source of socializing and fun. Get-togethers, referred to by the participants as "frolics," received the name because of what the adult attendees did with joy; they frolicked.

Perhaps the greatest enjoyment experienced came from inviting people to bring a dish for supper to someone's house with music and dancing afterward. The music would be live and provided by farmers and others who lived in the county.

My curious nature made me wonder why Sampson Waddell seemed to avoid wiping away the fiddle dust from his instrument. The high-use area of the fiddle had a covering of bow dust that seemingly was always there. I imagined Sampson thought it was bad luck to clean off the debris.

A person could not pick up the phone and dial everyone to invite them to a neighbor's house. They had to either run into them in town, drive by their house or ask someone to pass on the word. My observation was that most attendees were within a few miles of the party house, so if driving to notify partiers, the distance was short.

Places I remember congregating for these music sessions were Anderson Williams', Calvin Miller's, Sampson Waddell's homes, and Anderson's camp house which resided on the shore of Rock Pond. The building was all wood construction outside and inside with a rustic flair which made everyone feel at home as if they belonged there.

Attendees included the Ralph and Hardy Horne families, Miller families, Wilfred Tyler family, Bud Moulton family, Hunter families, Junior Bowen family, the band members' families and others that have faded in my memory. Twelve to fifteen people would be in attendance at a home and twenty-five or more at Anderson's camp house.

After everyone dug heartily into all the food brought by the various families, the bed would be removed from a bedroom to provide dancing space.

The square dance was the rage, and Daddy was a "caller" among his other talents. The caller yelled out "spin your partner," "do-si-do," which meant dancing back to back, "allemande" and other commands to the dancers.

The grownups had loads of good, clean fun when they spun around the room with the enticing spirit making me want to be old enough to dance. It was an excellent opportunity to catch up on each other's lives and to ask "How fat is the baby?" In spite of no phones, neighbors stayed "caught up" on each other's lives.

The best gatherings seemed to be when the group met at Anderson Williams' camp house. Long tables and benches for the food, socializing and enjoying the meals made the venue ideal for partying. The frolickers would become a raucous, noisy crowd. They may not have seen each other for a few weeks or days but still had lots of news and laughs to share. The food was plain ol' exquisite, down-home delicious.

During preparation for the meal, Daddy and Mr. Sampson set up their equipment outside in the open air: chairs, Daddy's amplifier, the instruments, and an extension cord. Oh! I almost forgot the most important piece of "equipment" from Daddy's perspective, a half pint of Early Times under the truck seat, where it stayed until it was time for a boost.

The band took a break about every thirty minutes when he would take a swig. Decorum of the time dictated that he always should drink behind a truck or tree and not in front of the ladies and children; Mama's rule as well. I noticed he had to get a few sessions under his belt before he would sing my favorite song, "50 cents," toward the end of the evening.

Some attendees brought their favorite chairs from home in the back of their trucks. They would position them in front of the band close or farther away according to their preferences and level of deterioration of hearing. During the band breaks, the chatter created a pleasant sound of people visiting and enjoying each other.

The band would go for a couple hours and run through the gamut of old songs in their repertoire: "Iron City Twist," "Bill Bailey," "Down Yonder," "Alabama Jubilee," "Mockingbird Hill," "Wabash Cannon Ball," "The Orange Blossom Special," "Your Cheatin' Heart," "Hey Good Looking" and many others that have passed from my mind. "Down Yonder," featuring Daddy and Dixie Maude, and Orange Blossom Special, featuring Sampson, were favorites of the crowd.

The Orange Blossom Special had Sampson on his fiddle stroking out the lively tune as good as anyone could play it. The wheels of the train turning, the smoke stack coughing, and the whistle blowing livened the audience. Sampson, a top notch fiddle player, was always humbled by the applause.

Having heard so many instrumental versions of "Down Yonder," I thought it was without lyrics. In the later '50s, Daddy started singing it, which brought much more meaning to the rendition.

In the early part of the evening, the children would start up a game of Hide and Seek or Kick the Can. We trounced all over the woods around the camp house but not once attacked by a critter. I don't remember anyone getting poison ivy, so a few scratches from briars or a thorny bush were the chief casualties of the fun.

For the younger readers who don't know what Kick the Can is. It involved stacking up three or four empty food cans. A player who was "It" would go into the woods to find someone who was hiding. Upon spotting a player, "It" would race back to the cans and kick them over before the other person got there. Then the "spotted player" was "It." If "It" went too far away from the cans, a player might see from the woods and sneak up to knock the cans over causing "It" to start all over again.

After we tired, we would go back to the folks and sit by our mamas as our eyes got heavy. Falling asleep proved a little difficult with the amplifier blasting away.

Around 10 o'clock the time came for the frolickers to call it a night and load themselves and everything they brought into the vehicles to drive home. Good-byes were exchanged, and everyone looked forward to the next time. Since most of these happenings occurred on Saturday night, the adults would have a day of rest the next day.

The fraternization during the events created a "tightness" of relationships that was unique to the era. People cared for and depended on each other with unspoken love. To have witnessed and be a part of the time, I consider a great blessing.

Daddy, Sampson and other players occasionally performed at the American Legion when farmers and townspeople came together for a special event. J B Clarke told me a few years ago he really enjoyed Daddy's mandolin playing on those occasions.

It is hard to believe that these remembrances are from fifty-five years ago. The happenings remain so meaningful and crystal clear in my mind, they could have transpired only twenty years back. I can still hear the cicadas (locusts) chirping, the frogs croaking, the laughter of the people, the music, the moss hanging from the oaks, and the damp night air soaked with the Rock Pond smells.

Everything has a beginning and an ending. On a day in the late '60s or early '70s, Sampson played his fiddle for the last time. Daddy had a stroke when he was seventy-six that inhibited his ability to read. The Lord left him with the gift of music. He continued to play his mandolin until the last year when he passed at the age of eighty-two in 1990. He would miss a chord occasionally, and I could see the disappointment on his face. With music in his soul, he loved the feel of that instrument in his hands and being the master of the wonderful sounds it made.

Dixie Maude, quite a lady and the youngest of the group, passed on approximately ten or fifteen years ago. Randall Williams who was the husband of my aunt Iris Trawick Williams was her brother.

In 2015 Atwood Lane, past ninety-five in years and a WWII veteran, was the only surviving member of the band and resided in Seminole Nursing Home. Still getting around with failing eyesight and he was occasionally seen in one of the local restaurants. God bless him. Thanks for the memories and thanks for his service to our country.

Down-home carved out a piece of rural Georgia that will forever be remembered by those who were a part of it. Fleeting away as many things good and wholesome, it left a strong heritage.

20

Figs and First Friend

In the 1950s fig trees could be found at most houses especially in the country. The tasty fruit remained an important staple in breakfast diets. Biscuits, fig preserves, grits, eggs and bacon comprised a delectable, hearty farm breakfast savored by families.

We would fork a fig and place it on the edge of a buttered biscuit, and then bite fig and biscuit together. Or we would insert figs inside of a buttered biscuit to make a small fig sandwich. The fig syrup we sopped similarly as cane syrup. Coming home from school starved and making a fig sandwich with mayo could calm an appetite. Yummy!

Mama always preserved about seventy-five pint jars of figs for the coming year. We would all gather around the tree to fill pans and buckets with figs. Mama cautioned us to not pick those that were too ripe since they did not make the best preserves. She preferred the less ripe, firm ones. If I were hungry, I ate a bellyful of the riper ones while picking.

Fig poison and wasp nests came with the territory. The white fig "milk" from a broken leaf could get on our hands and lower arms causing a rash. When we found a wasp nest, we would usually leave the nearby figs for the blue jays and mockingbirds. Often I would go back after the picking and tear down the nest, so we would not have to be bothered the next time.

Mama processed the figs in two or three "cookings" using a large amount of sugar to get the sweet preserve taste. The smell of the figs cooking on the stove in large pans made the mouth water for the first fresh-preserve breakfast.

Old Stuff, Newer Stuff, and Stuff

Granddaddy Mills left two fig trees on our farm. One stood behind the barn and the other was closer to the house and adjacent to a chinaberry tree which we used for shade. They produced an abundance of figs, so we had a few cousins that would come by to pick them.

The tree closest to our house shielded from sight the first outhouse I remember. It sat behind the tree and close to it creating a private location for us to "do a job" as we used to refer to it. It had been left by Granddaddy Mills and had aged almost beyond serviceability having handled its share of jobs. The door had lost part of its moorings, so it had to be dragged open and closed.

When I was five years old, Edwina Hand Skipper and her parents lived down the road about a quarter mile on Bud and Lila Youmans' farm. Back from the war, Ed Hand struggled as a many young men did getting his bearings and figuring out a means of "making it." I remember a long knife, probably a machete that he brought back from the war, which was impressive and put fear in my soul. It was the biggest knife I had seen.

On a few occasions Edwina and I played together; one of the more poignant memories included our outhouse. She called it having to go shoo-shoo. I would follow along, and she would close the door tightly afraid that I would see. Such innocence we shared when contrasted with the cold, cruel world we both would have to confront as we grew.

One day my dog Dash got me into a heap of trouble. I like to blame it on Dash but know I was a willing accomplice, probably the ring leader. Dash and I would roam the ditches along the then dirt road by our house looking for rat holes. Dash would dig them out as I stood by cheering him on. His method was to dig a few strokes, take a sniff of the hole to see how close he was to the "prize," and then dig deeper. Soon there would be a brief rustle of activity as the mouse tried to bound from the bottom of his hole. Dash would quickly put the "chomps" on him and spit him on the ground.

That day we kept going down the ditches toward Edwina's house, and eventually I decided to go visit her. We arrived, and she came out to play but not for long. Mama came walking up the road carrying a switch. Neither a pretty nor welcome sight. Trouble was brewing, and I was the main attraction. She had lost her little boy and had come to retrieve him with a stern reminder not to leave the house again. My worst nightmare was about to arrive in the flesh.

In a fit of temporary insanity, I told her she was not going to whip me; I was going to whip her, a mistake of gargantuan proportions. In a matter of seconds, I tried to think of plan B, but it was hard to concentrate with that switch hitting my legs every few milliseconds. It seemed she laid to me all of that quarter mile trip back home. My accomplice Dash, being Scot free, trotted along with a smug look, unimpressed by my inability to tolerate a little pain.

That is it for figs and a friend circa 1950. Edwina became a friend for life, and I still love the taste of fig preserves. Thank God for beautiful memories and long lasting friends.

21

Raising the Kids

When I was a child, there were a large number of "sayings" that were repeated over and over by parents or other adults. Parents would prefer to believe what they say goes in one ear and out the other but not necessarily so. Below is a partial list:

> Honesty is the best policy.
> A penny saved is a penny earned.
> He, who laughs last, laughs best.
> You get out of it what you put into it.
> If you want something done right, do it yourself.
> Waste not, want not.
> Work is its own reward.
> Cleanliness is next to Godliness.
> People who live in glass houses should not throw stones.
> Necessity is the mother of invention.
> If you tell one lie, you will have to tell another one to cover it up.
> Do it right, or you will have to lick your calf over.
> You can tell a person by the company he keeps.
> Do it right or do it again.
> There is a time and a place for everything.
> A stitch in time saves nine.
> Don't put off until tomorrow what can be done today.
> Always save for a rainy day.
> Clean around your own back door first.

Spare the rod, spoil the child.
Anything worth having is worth taking care of.
Better late than never.
The squeaky wheel gets the grease.
The grass is always greener on the other side of the fence.
The two things that can always be separated are a fool and his money.

When I was growing up, I heard the expressions over and over from Mama and Daddy and others. If they had not made an impression, I would not have remembered them. The sayings taught character traits: frugality, honesty, independence, importance of a quality job, hygiene, the positives of work, importance of good friends, timeliness, not to judge people, discipline and conservation of time. They gave us values and bearings, the direction of "true North." We heard these because our parents heard them from their parents.

For whatever cultural reasons, these are not heard nearly as much now as then. The partial demise of these character traits in our society has weakened our country. "Culture creep," good or bad, will always be with society.

22

Gasoline

Over a lifetime I have witnessed tremendous changes in the sale of gasoline to the consumer and the service associated. The transition has traveled the gamut from the proprietor pumping the gas and the consumer taking care of everything else to the consumer pumping the gas and being responsible for all car maintenance.

When we bought gas at Emmett Ward's store in Iron City in the '50s, he came outside and pumped it. Forget the windshield. If we wanted it cleaned, the responsibility belonged to us.

In the late '50s and into the early '60s, the large oil companies would have gas wars. It was not uncommon for a war to break out in Donalsonville and/or Iron City which offered twenty-five percent or greater discounts to the going price for the area during a few weeks of intense competition. An attempt by the oil companies to gain market share drove the price wars. The effectiveness was doubtful, so eventually they went the way of the dodo bird.

In the heat of this competition, extra service for the consumer arose. Service stations were willing to clean the windshield and check fluid levels under the hood. Checking the oil could be profitable with many old "oil burners" on the road. The service attendant would show the oil stick to the customer for confirmation that he was "down a quart." Unscrupulous stations would have their attendants "short stick" the oil check to show a "fake low." Power steering and automatic transmission fluids could be sold as well via the look under the hood.

In the summer of 1963, Terry Ingram and I went to Tallahassee to live for the summer and work at my uncle's service stations. In those days young people knew not to quibble about the work, the hours or the money. We were glad to get the job and a modicum of cash flow.

Soon Terry and I learned that the service station business in the big city followed different management procedures. Each gas island had a vacuum system mounted for cleaning the floors of cars and trucks that came in for gas. When a customer drove up, the attendant would start the gas pumping and ask the driver if he wanted the car floors cleaned. It the answer was yes, we vacuumed the front and back areas. The ladies with prettier legs had cleaner floors.

After finishing the vacuuming, the attendant cleaned the windshield if the customer wanted the bugs removed. He would go to the front of the car, look at the driver, tap the hood, and expect a nod from the driver if looking under the hood was needed. If the driver wanted the fluid levels checked, we chiefly checked the oil. Optionally we checked the transmission and power steering fluids if the driver so desired.

We preferred the patrons in a hurry. They only wanted gas and to be gone which meant less work for us.

The cooling systems of the day had started requiring expensive coolants, so the radiator was not checked unless the driver insisted. When releasing the radiator cap, extreme care was applied to avoid a burn from escaping steam, and a small amount of coolant would be wasted on the ground.

If one attendant did all the above by himself, a car might take as long as ten minutes to get back on the road. With two attendants the time could be half that or less, depending on which services they wanted.

Terry and I got a good workout pumping gas, vacuuming, cleaning windshields, and checking fluids. If someone came in and wanted a ten dollar car wash, we took care of it and put a smile on their faces when they came back for the vehicle.

For forty-two dollars take home pay, we worked six-day weeks We recognized it was a starter job and certainly not where we intended to finish our careers. The position we viewed as part of growing up and learning to manage our lives, so we would not have to do that kind of work for a career.

Today with better built cars and a different nature of competition self-service everything is the norm. We do all of our own cleaning: windshields, interior, exterior. Fluid levels are not an issue on the newer vehicles. Regular visits to the dealership handle all of the maintenance issues. I cannot recall how many years ago I checked the fluid levels in my vehicle for the last time.

There has been quite an evolution in the car service and maintenance business over the last sixty or so years. Looking back at all the changes confirms to me progress was made. When adjusted for inflation, every service associated is performed more cheaply and better than back in the day.

23

The Pond

About a hundred and fifty yards down the road from our house, on Bud and Lila Mae Youmans's land, stood a growth of live oaks, turkey oaks, and mayhaw trees which we called the pond, encompassing about twenty-five acres.

The Pond lowland held at least a small amount of water in all times; in wet years water would cover its entire acreage. Heavy rains would create a large water drain which originated on Tom Trawick's farm, passed across a corner of our land and entered the pond via a culvert under HWY 285.

In my very early years, little did I know that the area was going to be a "character" in a play called "my life." It was the "star" of a large number of experiences and would always pull me back for more.

The oldest memory is of a large oak tree by the road which became a fun place to play. A Tarzan movie probably had motivated my two brothers to hang a chain from a very high limb in the tree. Lloyd being the oldest had shimmed out on a limb thirty feet in the air and secured the chain with which they could glide through the air like the Lord of the Jungle.

As it grew, the tree's main trunk had split into many other trunks fairly low to the ground, so with little effort they could climb it. One trunk had chosen to run almost parallel to the ground and had an eight or ten foot drop to the cushioned leaf floor of the forest.

Before I was old enough to risk a Tarzan feat, I would follow them to the tree and envy their fun.

The chain was long enough that its end could be reached from the ground, so it was easy to grab it and pull it over to the long horizontal trunk which set up a flying trip through the air. They would get the chain and walk along the trunk to a point where they had enough slack for a long swing. They would then jump off the trunk and swing thirty or forty feet before releasing and falling to the ground on their feet.

When I reached seven or eight years old, I was brave enough to swing too, but by then age had caused Lloyd and Jerome to lose interest.

The chain hung from the tree for about fifty years until fifteen or so years ago when the tree was burned in a clearing project. The chain had been a notch in my memory of long ago times and brought a tinge of sadness when I noticed it was gone.

The numerous mayhaw trees provided the berries for Mama to make jelly every spring. The fruit were easier to gather during high water when the berries floated on top and were easy to scoop up. In drier years they had to be picked up off the ground or from the trees. Mama always made forty or fifty jars of jelly for us to enjoy at breakfast with biscuits. Today I still enjoy it whether with loaf bread or biscuits—an unforgettable, delicious taste that refuses to diminish.

The pond left me with one troublesome memory that has stuck so vividly. Life on the farm was centered to an extent on food and the usefulness of the animals who received it. A three-legged bird dog named Gunner—with one front leg seriously injured—had been given to Daddy by one of his brothers. I was too young to understand why the transaction occurred but witnessed the results. A three-legged bird dog cannot hunt effectively as one with all its limbs.

One day Daddy told Jerome to take Gunner down to the Pond and "take care of him." Being six or seven years old, the request did not hit me with full force. Jerome grabbed the shotgun, called Gunner and headed toward the pond. In my childhood naiveté and innocence, I could not fully assimilate what was about to happen. Following along with Jerome to the Pond, Gunner tracked ahead thinking we were going hunting.

When we got to the edge of the woods, Jerome called Gunner, and he came running. Stopping ten or fifteen feet away, he awaited a command. Jerome shot him once in the head and he collapsed, instantly dead. He left him there for the buzzards.

The one incident taught me so much about the coldness and harshness of life. It was not an act I could have committed, but I tried to understand the necessity of it without success. Life was not going to always be fair to me or to others. One of my earliest lessons in the long school of completely understanding fairness indelibly etched a spot in my brain.

As I grew up, I learned the pond could supply so many things: fish bait, mayhaws, game, recreation, and solace.

When I was about eight years old, I brought home eight or ten bream fish in a bucket of water and released them when the water was high. In four or five years, the pond had become well stocked with fish. I had no idea how many until a dry spell in 1958 shrunk the water down to a small spot in the center. I observed hundreds of dead fish, buzzards, and an almost unbearable smell of decaying fish. If I had known how many fish there were, I would have been catching them.

When the water in the Pond was at a high level one year, I noticed tens of thousands of tadpoles around the edge of the water. When those tadpoles turned into frogs, thousands of them came forth. Having not witnessed a plague of frogs, I was amazed at the presence of little amphibians everywhere. They migrated up onto the road where they were crushed by cars creating "frog mush," an anomaly of nature that I would not witness again.

As I grew old enough to use a shotgun, I discovered plentiful game in the woods. Two coveys of quail ranged in the area which I would occasionally see in our field feeding. A number of them landed in Mama's pot and on our table for a delicious meal.

Doves liked to get water at the pond and roost in the oaks and mayhaw trees. Late in the afternoon I would harvest a few of them for the dinner table. To round out our game diet, I would shoot a few squirrels if dove and quail were hard to get or out of season.

Chief and I loved to visit the pond to chase rabbits. In only a few minutes, Chief and a rabbit would be on the run. We got a few, but they were pretty smart about going deep into brush piles where Chief could not get them. He would voice his displeasure with raucous barking, but we had to accept that Ol' Bugs had found security in his version of Uncle Remus's Briar Patch.

Today I can fully appreciate how fortunate it was to have a respite, a retreat in nature where I could rejoice, experience, and learn about life. With great granddaddy Joe Spooner having raised his brood only a half mile down the road, I can rest assured I was only one of many who experienced the treasures of the pond which had contributed to people's lives for generations

24

Kennith Fields

Kennith Fields (March 26, 1931 - July 8, 1950)

Occasionally, a character comes along who stands out so prominently people speak fondly of him seventy-five years later. Kennith Fields grew to be such a person whose personality and actions set him aside from the crowd.

Kennith was born in 1931 to Alma Spooner Fields, who lived in Iron City, GA. His father Henry E. Fields who his mother married in 1921 apparently left the stage during Kenneth's very young life. None of Kennith's school mates recalled a father being present. They lived in a home at the intersection of HWY 45 and the street running behind the Iron City Community Center where Kennith grew up adjacent to Iron City School.

Kennith, a sizable kid who was larger than all his class members because of missing a grade or two or more, wore overalls and seemed to constantly pursue the next batch of mischief to create.

Living near the school, he owned the job of firing up the boiler each morning. The boiler had a reservoir filled with water which helped add moisture to the dry winter air. Kenneth always carried kitchen matches in his back pocket for lighting the boiler.

A mimosa tree grew across the street from the school yard which had been trimmed leaving a "Y" fork shape. The trimmed tree put ideas in Kennith's head of fun to have.

Kenneth obtained a red rubber car inner tube which was common in those days. Being made from natural rubber, the tubes were sought out by young boys for use in slingshots. Rubber bands cut from these were excellent at propelling a rock from a slingshot thong. Slingshots were popular, so boys would walk around with them in their back pockets ready to strike whatever target they chose.

Kenneth cut the inner tube in half and secured one half to each of the Y forks of the tree. He fashioned and attached a suitable thong to the tube sections and behold he had a huge slingshot. Knocking down the "walls of Troy" from ancient history captured his imagination.

"Troy" was the school house filled with attacking hordes of teachers, so he began lobbing half bricks in that direction. A utility building on the near side of the school building bore the brunt of the blows. Care-free Kenneth waged "war" until the school principal interceded.

Kennith became the nemesis of every teacher who had the "no pleasure" of him attending their class. Being so incorrigible, one day when the teacher left the room, he peed in her chair and received one of the many whippings coming his way.

In the fourth grade Mrs. Marie Spooner, Rudolph's wife, had the misfortune of being his teacher. Rudolph apparently was a distant cousin to Kennith.

Kennith had a favorite torment of urinating in the reservoir of the boiler. As the boiler got hot, a putrid smell permeated the rooms. As Kennith sat in his chair and snickered, Marie would complain of how stuffy it was in the room and start opening windows

Once Kennith had fully tested Miss Marie's patience causing her to administer a whipping. Offering no cooperation and being as big as she was, she requested Principal Bentson to hold him. After much huffing and puffing, Bentson put a hold on Kennith, and Miss Marie set about applying the rod to his butt.

All of a sudden smoke started rising, but it was not Kennith's butt, at least not directly. The strokes of the rod had ignited the kitchen matches in Kennith's back pocket. Now they all danced around trying to smother the fire. Kennith danced more than they since he had more to lose; an eventful day at Iron City School to be long remembered.

Whether Kennith finished high school is uncertain. The Korean Conflict was in full surge when he joined the Army and went to the battle front. His fate was to never see Iron City again being killed in action shortly after joining the battle and his body not recovered.

In the 1950s I had observed a small grave marker in Rock Pond Cemetery with a picture of him in his uniform, the dates of birth and death, and the letters "MIA." Being a curious sort, Kennith and his fate were held in my mind to not be forgotten.

Recently I had taken a couple walks through the graveyard looking for his marker, but it was not to be found in its original location. Guessing that it was moved adjacent to his mother's grave since she died many years after him, I enlisted my friend Terry Ingram who is an expert at genealogy to find where she was buried.

Terry learned that Alma who lived to be eighty-three years old was buried in Oliver Grove Cemetery next to her first husband Waller Murphy who only lived to be twenty-four years of age. Kennith's marker I found a few feet away with his picture on it which is shown above. Alma married three times so being buried by her first husband seemed unusual. Another oddity: Julia Martha Spooner, Alma's mother was buried at the left end of the Murphy plot. Her husband George Jasper (Jap) Spooner was buried in a separate Rock Pond plot.

Presumably Alma resided in the house in Iron City until her death. She lived a life of solitude and could be seen walking around town since she had no vehicle. She passed in 1974, and the house was torn down eventually.

Thanks to my cousin Edgbert Williams, a story teller in his own right, for relating most of the above regarding Kennith. It is always delightful to have him and wife Pat to lunch and listen to his old stories.

Thanks to Jimmy Hornsby for sharing the story of the giant slingshot.

Both Jimmy and Edgbert spoke fondly of Kennith and expressed their appreciation of his sacrifice for our country. He was on this earth only a brief period, but he left a mark and he left memories. God bless his soul.

25

Sharecropping

In the early part of the twentieth century, sharecropping was a way of life for many families with it phasing in as tenant farming disappeared. A few land owners had huge amounts of land, so In absence of the mechanization, which is prevalent today, a large quantity of labor had to be secured to do the massive amount of work.

There were two ways chiefly to manage a large farm: the use of tenant farmers or sharecropping. The tenant farmers were essentially "owned" by the proprietor of the land. They and their families lived on his land and worked for him at his will. Pay consisted of a meager house to live in, a small amount of cash and food. Food often consisted of a place to have a garden and possibly a small quantity of livestock.

With this kind of leverage held by the landowner, they were slightly above slave status in some cases. Tenant farmers lived a sparse life until tractors eventually replaced the mule and plow. Mechanization displaced large numbers of tenant farmers from the land and into towns or cities.

In the 1930s and 1940s, Peter Cummings owned land around Lela, across the road from Bartow Gibson's home. A railroad came through the town, making it a thriving community. A commissary store, still standing, provided the tenants the basic food needs: sugar, flour, meal, salt, lard, rice, beans, etc. In the 1950s the buildings were still in place, but since then the bulk have disappeared.

My grandfather Mills was a tenant farmer in the area of Ashford, Alabama during the late nineteenth and early twentieth centuries. Several of his younger children including Daddy were born while on the farm.

Living with them in his later years, was my great grandfather William Mills, who served in the Civil War.

My grandmother Mills inherited a sum of money when an aunt died, which provided funds for them to move to Seminole County (then Decatur County) and purchase fifty acres of land about a mile west from Rock Pond. This land was ample for them to finish raising their family while farming with mules and surviving well for the period.

When I was a kid, we owned the fifty acres of land which my father had bought after my grandfather died. As a four-year-old child, I can remember taking my father a glass of milk in the field while he was plowing with a mule.

Soon it became obvious tractor farming was going to be the only way to survive going forward. Clyde, our very senior mule, was going to get a rest. After Daddy bought the tractor, she only helped plow and plant the garden.

Daddy had already started sharecropping with my great uncle Howard Spooner during the last few years that he farmed our land with the mule. With Uncle Howard owning a John Deere tractor, operating it gave Daddy the confidence to buy his own C Farmall in circa 1950 or 1951. He was excited to ride the tractor and not walk behind Clyde with the dust and occasional surprise, solid and gas, she passed.

The finer details of how the sharecropping agreement worked escape me. I know that a relative furnished the land and half the fertilizer and seed. Daddy was responsible for the other half and the tractor work and labor associated with planting and gathering the crop. The revenue from the harvest they split equally. With the entire agreement sealed by a handshake, Daddy sharecropped with relatives: Howard Spooner, Bud Youmans, Gordon Spooner, Raymond Simmons and George Trawick.

Sharecropping gave us the ability to farm a total of approximately one hundred acres. Our farm had cotton and peanut allotments of roughly twelve acres each with the amount of the allotments controlled by the Department of Agriculture. The balance of the land was in corn and pasture for hogs, the milk cow, and our mule until she died.

We would sharecrop roughly twenty-five acres each of corn and peanuts. Informal agreements helped both parties; e.g., our relative would loan us a few pieces of equipment to farm, and we would help with odd jobs in their operation. I remember helping treat sheep with a pink solution squirted down their throats when George Trawick had a herd. With him being the only "sheep baron" in the area, we wondered, "Why the sheep?"

My next older brother Jerome quit working on the farm when I was about eleven or twelve years old. After that, Daddy and I did most of the work. Around that time, the cotton combine came into good functionality, and Daddy hired someone to pick our cotton which took a huge load off of us.

The cotton chopping, peanut hoeing, and weed pulling kept us busy with a small amount of hired help. By then tractors pulled mechanical peanut combines along "windrows" of peanut vines to harvest the nuts. We hired a relative who owned a peanut picker to harvest our peanuts.

Getting corn into the barn was hard work until the conveyor-elevators came into use. We previously had to shovel the corn out of a trailer and toss it into the barn with a seed fork. Using the elevator, we could push it off the back of the trailer onto the conveyor, and it would transport the corn into the barn.

We lived in a sharecropper house until I finished high school. The home was there when my granddaddy bought the farm and possibly built by my great granddaddy Joe Spooner. The road by our house had several old tenant/sharecropper houses built on the same floor plan. There were two on the hill east of our house, one about two hundred yards west of our house, two across the road from Bud Youmans' land, one adjacent to Uncle Bud and Aunt Lila Mae's house, and one about a mile west of our house where I caught the school bus for ten years. The number of the houses gave confirmation of the quantity of labor required to farm land in those times. These old testaments of days gone by are history now, victims of progress and the changing economics of farming.

As I reminisce, I can appreciate sharecropping more than I did at the time. It helped provide a home for our family in a great community of relatives. We children learned about hard work, and its role in having a full life.

It was by no means a good living as regard to material things. Seeing other people with "luxuries" I would like to have one day proved a great motivator for the rest of my work life.

Knowing hard work was preventive medicine, we did not go to bed hungry. The challenging experiences, with which I would never want to part, are etched comfortably in my mind and are "old friends" who help tell me who I am.

26

Paul Raymond Evans

Who Was Paul Raymond Evans?

His name is etched on the Vietnam Memorial monument in front of our courthouse in Donalsonville. Probably I am the only person in the area that knows much about Raymond, but his memory will forever reside with me. I knew Paul Raymond Evans and am proud to say I did.

Raymond was the son of Gwendolyn Adams Evans, who was the daughter of Edna Trawick Adams and John E. Adams. Edna was the daughter of Emory Arthur Trawick and Chloe Alma Spooner and my mother's sister, the oldest in that Trawick family. John E, who served in WWI, was brother to the late Sweetzer Adams and related to John Quincy Adams.

Gwendolyn and her two sisters Maxine and Joan spent the major portion of their younger years in Seminole County. The youngest daughter Duane was three when they left the county. John E. and Edna had a small farm adjacent to Paul and Ethel Moseley's place near Iron City.

Edna and John E. eventually moved to Jacksonville, Florida, after living in Perry, Florida for a period, but they both remained members of the Olive Grove Primitive Baptist Church making several trips each year to attend services and visit with our family.

When John E. retired in about 1958, they moved back to Seminole County. Paul Moseley sold them an acre of land on which they built a small house. Eventually Edna's failing health caused them to sell the house and move back to Florida to live with Raymond's mother circa 1965.

Raymond's mother Gwendolyn loved Rock Pond Church and came back occasionally with her mother to visit. She brought Raymond, her daughter Sandi and daughter Angie. Raymond was the same age as I with Sandi about a year and a half younger and Angie five plus years younger.

Raymond, Sandi and I played together when they came in the mid to late '50s. They were my first city friends and different. I could tell right away they had not experienced the rough and tumble upbringing common with the Mills kids. They were polite, presented themselves well, articulate and used a different vocabulary than I. A mole about the size of a dime Raymond had on his cheek distinguished him along with the blonde hair and blue eyes.

We all got along well and had a lot of fun together. Soon I was dragging them across the fields and into the woods and showing them sights they had not seen before. Sandi continues to tell me how well she liked the old house I was raised in and the farm environment. She failed to become friends with the outhouse. She was always afraid something from below was going to rise up and bite a tender spot. She holds a sharp memory of ant hills and fireworks, mischief I trained them in.

It seemed that Raymond thoroughly enjoyed himself. He and his sisters had lived the "military brat" experience since birth. He could have probably told me more about the world than I could have shown him on the farm. Jacksonville, Florida, Fort Campbell Kentucky, and Washington, DC were three of the many places they had resided in the states.

Ray Evans, his father, had a distinguished military career in the Navy serving through half of WWII, all of the Korean Conflict and half of Vietnam. He was an enlisted man for twelve years and was commissioned in Officers Candidate School within a two month period in 1955. Captaining the USS Papago based out of Norfolk, VA, he served during the missile crisis in the early '60s. The vessel was in the Cuba area when the crisis began and stayed for four more weeks when it ended.

When Raymond and I parted circa 1958 and said goodbye, I had no idea that would be the last time I would see him. The next time I heard of Raymond was in 1968 when in college. I received a letter from Mama stating that Raymond had been killed in Vietnam. Being in college and having meager funds, it was impossible to make his funeral in Jacksonville.

Raymond's death hung heavily on me. My memory of him from age twelve made it difficult to imagine him as a Marine. In his youth he came across as such a nice, agreeable, non-combative young fellow. Eight years later he was a man and prepared to give his life for his country.

Raymond had attended two years of school at Louisburg Junior College at Louisburg, NC, where he was active in the Young Republicans Club. For a reason which only he knew, he chose to join the Marines on June 4, 1966, his twenty-first birthday. Not one word of his intentions had been mentioned to his father or mother beforehand. Receiving a call from Raymond and being told he had enlisted, the family knew most Marines served in Vietnam, so fear was in their hearts. After basic training at Camp

Lejeune, NC, he came home for one visit, with his family never to see him again.

He tried to call home once with so much irony attached. He had been on R&R in Hong Kong. When the phone rang at his mother's house, his aunt happened to be the one that answered. She said that she thought a nut from China had misdialed and hung up, not knowing Raymond was in the country. His last chance to talk to his mother ended abruptly with a dial tone.

Raymond was in L Co., 3rd battalion, 27th Marines. He was an infantryman and very proud of receiving a battlefield promotion to corporal before the promotion based on service came through.

He was killed in night action in the field May 5, 1968, due to shrapnel wounds. The wounds were so severe that the casket was not opened for the family. Sandi stated, "It made it that much harder. We could not really say goodbye." He was buried in Jacksonville, FL.

Now, to why his name is on our courthouse monument. When he enlisted, his military parents lived in Alexandria, Virginia. He knew he had no permanent address for military records which caused him to use his grandparent's address, Iron City, Georgia. Later his father had his records changed to show he was born at the Naval Hospital in Jacksonville, so his name could be added to the Veteran's Memorial in Tallahassee.

His parents had his body moved to Woodlawn Cemetery, Perry, Florida after his father retired.

The city has a memorial park in Perry where a patriotic ceremony is held each Memorial Day. They raise a flag that was on a veteran's coffin, and it flies for a year. Raymond's flag was chosen for the 2014 year.

His father lived in Perry until his passing as does currently his sister Sandi with his sister Angie nearby at St. Augustine, Florida. His mother passed away a few years back. Sandi said Ray wore his navy uniform at the local Memorial Day services and looked great; he still had the slim frame of when he retired.

That is the story of the patriot, Paul Raymond Evans, an exceptionally man who loved his country. May God bless him and his family. He is still remembered, and his service will not be forgotten. Neither will the blond-haired, blue-eyed boy who tramped the fields of Seminole County with me.

Note: (Written by Sandi Evans Oller, Raymond's sister, on May 5, 2017)

On May 5, 1968, my brother, Marine Corporal Paul Raymond Evans was killed in action in Viet Nam. He would have been twenty-two years old on June 4. Raymond joined the Marines at a time when men were leaving the country rather than serve. He knew that as a Marine, he probably wouldn't make it home alive. But he joined anyhow. He didn't hold his breath, hoping that he wouldn't get drafted. He joined so that he could do his share in the fight for freedom.

I recently found some papers that described the battle he was killed in. Every man in his unit was killed except one, and that's because he wasn't in that battle. A few weeks later the man was gravely injured, but he did survive.

Witnesses said Raymond was doing all he could to help his men before he was ripped apart by shrapnel. He went into the battle as a Lance Corporal, but was promoted to Corporal after the battle. Everyone who saw the battle described Raymond as a hero, but knowing him, I doubt he felt that way; he was a hero.

All of our members of the military are heroes, in their own way. We think of those fighting battles, but forget about the "behind the scenes" people, from those who prepared and served meals to those who handled the necessary paperwork to keep our military functioning.

If Raymond had lived, he would have been greeted by jeers, people calling him names, even physically assaulting him. That's how things were in 1968. We must never let this happen again. When you see a man or woman in uniform, just say, "Thank you for your service." Because they are all heroes, no matter what their job is, and they deserve to be recognized. And don't forget our veterans who have already served. Semper Fi!

27

Hard Fall

Fate can wield a severe blow to a small percentage of people, to an even smaller percentage when one of us is eighteen years old. Providence, an equal opportunity purveyor of misfortune, has no bias against any race, religious preference, age group, or other factor. As lightning, it strikes in seemingly a random fashion and changes lives forever. Thus was the case with Sidney Ingram.

In the first grade at Iron City School, Sid and I first became friends. Sid, a pudgy, laid back, easy going type of fellow got along with everyone. Wrestling and other physical encounters were not his forte being quick with a smile and a friend to all.

His father Tom carpentered, and his mother worked at the school lunch room; both honest, hard working, and solid citizens pounding out a living in the 1950s. They lived in a modest house in Iron City maybe a quarter mile from the center of town and had another child Tommy about six years older.

A couple of times in the second grade I visited him at his house for the day, and we enjoyed playing whatever town boys played in those days. I recall the visits but cannot say what we did together. When I started school in Donalsonville in the third grade, our paths diverged as he remained in Iron City School.

At the beginning of the eighth grade, Sid came back into my life somewhat. We were all in a struggle to make it through high school and had common experiences. He hung around with different kids than I. My memory is that he did not pass the eighth grade and was one year behind me for the rest of the time at SCHS.

Around Sid's junior year his brother gave him a Model T (my best guess) since I had no skills of recognizing old cars. It was hard enough to keep up with the newer models and the drastic changes in styling and performance with each year's offering. The car attracted girls like the liberal party attracts bad judgment. Whenever I saw him and the car, it seemed to be loaded with girls and guys to the point of hanging out the side and the back. The car, Sid, and the gang showed up at all events such as parades.

During the eleventh and twelfth grades, Sid spent substantial time at the radio station located across the road from the Cypress Park swimming pool. He had an opportunity to sit behind the microphone as did a few others and seemed to be a natural with the gift of gab a DJ requires. He soon was spending more and more time at the station.

Circa April, 1964, bad karma came tiptoeing in Sid's direction. Fate doesn't get on a loud speaker and announce it is coming. Always arriving unexpectedly in a fleeting moment, it does the damage or good. The year after I finished high school, I worked in Atlanta, and Sid was to graduate in May.

One afternoon Sid had left the station in a small sports car with Joe Wingate driving and headed south on HWY 39. A man walking who had been drinking heavily stumbled from the shoulder into the road, and the car had a tremendous impact.

The windshields on those vehicles, especially small sports cars, were not sturdy as compared to those on today's vehicles. The body propelled across the hood and crashed into the windshield striking Sid head to head with tremendous force. The man was either dead at the scene or soon afterward, and Sid incurred a traumatic head injury with Joe having little or no injuries.

The doctors and Sid had to fight for his life. As I understood it, his body had to be packed in ice to control brain swelling. Brain surgery was scheduled to save his life.

Not long after he got home from an extended stay in the hospital, I visited him at his parents' home. One glance told me Sid had been through crippling trouble and pain. He had lost weight from his already slim frame, and his feet revealed the effects of being packed in ice. Parts of both feet had been removed with some toes amputated and flesh missing in the arch of his feet.

He was alive and recovering for which he had God to thank. He appeared to have a great attitude and had accepted his condition.

Left with a large scar in the center of his forehead and a different gait, he made the best of the "die which had been cast." Other than that, he apparently made a full recovery.

Unfortunately, going forward he had sensitive feet which required periodic medical care. As he has gotten older, foot pain has worsened.

Since then, I did not see him again until our 2015 class reunion. He and his wife were doing well, and it was great to see them.

He had a successful career in broadcasting and is now retired living in Brunswick, Georgia. After the broadcasting, he ran a charter boat operation for a few years. A stroke in 1994 slowed him down somewhat, and he has the continuing problem with his feet.

His wife Pat sent me an email, and we stay in contact on Facebook. They can be reached at pingram@actionac.com.

God bless Sid and Pat. Fate took a good whack at him, but he was able to have the career he wanted and a good life. Often fate is not that accommodating.

28

Red Devils and War Eagles

In the seventh grade (1957) Chester Lee our principal and Edward Everett, one of our two teachers, coached interclass football teams: the Red Devils and the War Eagles.

The Red Devils had team members Robert Lewis, Buz Guterman, Philip Baxley, Sidney Doster, Terry Ingram, Marshall Singletary, me, and others I cannot remember. Forgive my fuzzy memory. Buz and Terry alternated at quarterback, and Robert and I were halfbacks. Reuben Roberts, Leonard Spooner and Jimmy Glawson were on the War Eagles team.

There were cheerleaders from our class as well; Pat Sirmons, Judy Jenkins, Glenda Hawkins, Linda Reynolds, Carol Ann Owens, Sandra Ward and Shirley Phillips to name a few. I cannot remember all who cheered or for which team.

We were provided the uniforms: helmet, shoulder pads, jersey, and pants. No shoes. Someone did not understand the importance of shoes, but I guess they were not in the budget. I had no tennis shoes, so I went barefoot along with at least Robert Lewis. We had not played football in tennis shoes, so we did not know it was a handicap. Those who had no shoes were fleet of foot, but the drawback was getting your foot stepped on by a shoed player.

The first time on the practice field I felt like "robo football player." Overwhelmed by the bulky equipment hanging on while running and being so small and skinny, it felt like the uniforms swallowed us.

Mr. Everett, the Red Devils' coach, exposed the team to play-schematics and play-numbers. The 48 single wing was my favorite. Since I was right halfback, the quarter back tossed the ball back and I ran to the right with the rest of the backfield blocking.

The Red Devils won both games we played at Gibson Field. Undefeated, we showed the War Eagles who was tougher. A rematch could be arranged if they begged hard enough. A few walkers and Hovarounds will clutter the field if we don't do it soon.

That was my last meaningful experience with sports since participation proved impossible being Daddy's last child, and he depended on me for help with farming.

The two touchdowns I scored were my legacy of sorts. Mama rarely attended anything at school, but she showed up at one game after I ran a sixty-five yard touchdown. The ladies in the stands at the old Gibson Field told her, and she was so disappointed of missing her little boy's tiny moment of glory.

29

Donalsonville Elementary School Food

In 1953 when I entered the third grade, a small white cinder block lunchroom sat in the southwest corner of the campus. It was very similar to the one at Iron City but maybe twice the size. It had the usual food line with everyone accepting what was offered and gobbling it down. Rejection of food types was not a good alternative since a confrontation with hunger could be a real danger and to be wisely avoided.

The fast food of the '70s and beyond combined with poor parenting helped develop the "picky" behavior we read and hear about in today's school lunchrooms.

I remember racing every day to be near the front of the lunch line, a practice which probably has disappeared with culture change.

The quantity of food dipped onto my plate became my only issue. At home Mama placed big bowls of food on the table, and I loaded up my plate as if it was my last meal ever. Everything Mama said was food and she placed on the table I ate and enjoyed with zero complaints. Now I was stuck with these sectioned plates, and what I would call "a little bit" in each partition. It was barely enough because I don't remember going back to class with visions of pork chops dancing in my head. Growing like a weed, I could not be filled up anyhow. Weighing only one hundred forty-five pounds at six feet tall when I finished high school offered proof that I was a food-disposal unit.

Occasionally, I would sneak across the road to Goree's if I happened to get an extra dime. The "forbidden fruit" of an RC Cola and moon pie never tasted so good as when it came from the small store. The risk of being caught added to the adventure. A few fellow classmates would go down one block south and walk in behind the store, great exercise for the overly cautious. Crossing at the light with a few other kids brought me access to the world of forbidden goodies.

Periodically, Mr. Lee would herd Goree customers to his office and give them a good scaring, probably not spanked. He was such a sweet man students could not help but like him.

What we did on rainy days is not in my memory bank. The lunch room was the better part of a hundred yards from the school, or so it seemed. Everything was larger and distances were longer when we were eight years old. Did we just get wet? I don't remember raincoats? Way back in the deep vestiges of my mind I hold a fuzzy memory of walking to the lunch room with classmates holding a long sheet of plastic over our heads. I wonder of its accuracy.

In the community I came from, rain protection was an alien word. "Rubbers" worn by city children referred to the rubber covers worn over shoes, not the "socially beneficial" ones the older boys wore out in their billfolds.

Circa 1955 they built the combination lunch room-auditorium building on the west end of the school, a welcome addition. We could enter the building by simply walking down the hall without getting wet on rainy days. Assembly and class plays were the chief school functions of the auditorium while the eating area enjoyed use for both elementary and high school banquets and functions.

We had the same "un-full" plates. By use of the "licking trick," the last little bit could be had with a tilt of the plate and passing it along the tongue. No food was wasted that got near me, part of my raising. The kids of the era could have been well fed on what is wasted in today's school lunchrooms.

Mrs. Claudia Mae Owens and Mrs. Evelyn Hill cooked the food and always added a touch of love. They were good, honest, hard working ladies who did a wonderful job for the kids and with a pleasant demeanor; queens in their own realm. Claudia Mae's cinnamon roll recipe, stilly yummy, can be tasted on occasions at her daughter Jo's restaurant in Donalsonville.

The old lunchroom, the site of choice for fights, was not razed until years later. "Meet me behind the lunchroom" was the preamble to settling "imagined" differences. The sixth and seventh graders chiefly indulged in the fisticuffs. The hormones would start flowing, and they wanted to "whup somebody" to display their physical superiority while massaging their weak egos. The fighters had not yet learned one of the most important of lessons; someone always comes along who is stronger, bigger, and a better fighter than you.

Occasionally my good friend with small arms and hands would make up an excuse to go to the bathroom to enhance our diets when we were in the seventh grade. A few minutes later he would return with packages of Tom's toasted peanuts having learned to reach up into the machine and pull them out. He transferred this skill to the drink machine where he would reach up into the drop chute, flip a switch and out came a Nehi orange. Now we were ready to pour the nuts into the drinks at recess. What a treat! I will not mention his last name but it rhymed with modem.

We all were fed in this very simple world with no one in the federal bureaucracy trying to micromanage our diets. We ate what was offered and were glad to get it. Food was not taken for granted. Perhaps the abundance of offerings today has complicated the problem. In today's world, a large variety of food choices have helped create some picky eaters.

30

JT Lane's (Alf's Grandfather) Iron City Store, 1898

Alf Greene

On April 29, 2017, Connie and I visited the Greenes, a meeting which was my first opportunity to become acquainted. Having known of Alf for most of my life, it had been an arms-length association never affording a chance to get to know him. Alf and his loving wife Geanette live in the oldest house in Iron City which was built by a Dr. Jefferson Davis Chason circa 1885. Dr. Chason and his wife had nine children born in Iron City, so he built a sturdy, roomy house which has had longevity.

As our conversation began, I became confused because I thought he was talking about the Dr. Thomas J. Chason who practiced in Donalsonville and delivered many of my relatives, but he was referring to a Dr. Jefferson Chason who was Thomas's brother. The Dr. Jefferson Chason (February 24, 1861-October 30,1918) who sold the Iron City house to Alf's granddaddy JT Lane, on Alf's mother's side of the family, circa 1900 had Bainbridge roots and moved there to establish Riverside Hospital with his brother Dr. Gordon Chason. Riverside hospital ceased business years ago.

As we discussed JT Lane, Alf stated that Lane came from Twilight up toward Colquitt. I asked where and what it was. Circa 1900 it was a thriving community with a post office and located near Lane's bridge. Having not traveled to Lane's bridge, I made a note to maybe find it one day. Alf said Twilight is essentially gone today.

Learning of Alf's Lane roots, I told him we were distant kin since my great grandmother was a Lane. His wife joked that everyone in Seminole County is related except her because she came from Orlando.

When I asked Alf to tell the origin of the Greene family, he indicated Pine Mountain, Georgia and Cherokee County. His granddaddy farmed but developed a foot problem, and his doctor advised him to no longer follow a mule plowing the rocky soil of the area.

Eventually, Grandpa Greene moved his family including his wife, four or five boys and three girls, to Atlanta. He spent a year in the grocery business around the start of the twentieth century. Alf's father Earnest was born in 1898 around that time. Fearing his sons were going to get into trouble in the city, the senior Greene moved the family again after about a year.

Grandpa moved the family's possessions by railcar to Moultrie, Georgia, where he bought a large two story house. The house remained in the family for over a century, and one of Alf's cousin's daughters renovated it, and turned it into a bed and breakfast. It was sold roughly seven years ago to an individual outside the Greene family.

Alf's father Earnest found his way to Iron City where he started an egg business in 1927, with Alf being born in 1928. The major portion of his eggs came from chickens in the backyards on farms. The farm boys would remove eggs sometimes from setting chickens which had been fertilized. Jabo King and Weyman Cannington both ran rolling stores and would trade for chickens and eggs which they sold to Earnest. When Earnest opened some of the boxes of eggs, he found live chicks peeping inside which had hatched probably from the heat of the summer. He would finish raising the chickens and then sell them which got him into the beginnings of the chicken broiler business.

One of the pioneers of volume egg business in Seminole County was Booge Roberts' wife Lura Spooner Roberts. Alf related that she had two to three hundred laying chickens. She ventured into the egg business before Bud Youmans started in the middle '50s. With Bud's employment at Bartow Gibson's Roadside Milling, he had ready access to feed for his poultry.

Alf said a man named Jesse Jewell started the broiler business in North Georgia, so Earnest began driving up there to buy live chickens and bringing them back to Iron City for dressing. Eventually the broiler business started up in the South Georgia/North Florida/Southeast Alabama area, and Earnest could access live chickens closer to Iron City.

Alf and his wife both recalled stories of how stores in the area and in South Florida, where she was from, would have chickens in a pen in the back of their stores, affording their customers the opportunity to choose a chicken which the store owner would dress for them.

Being only seventeen, Alf stated that he missed WWII by six months since the war practice was to draft at eighteen years old. He was not to be so lucky with the Korean Conflict.

Earnest had insisted on Alf getting a college education, so he earned a business degree at Mercer University in Macon, Georgia. After finishing, he was drafted to serve during the Korean Conflict. With his college degree, the army placed him at Fort Jackson, South Carolina for the duration working in an office. Serving his two years, he returned to Iron City.

Alf remembered three people from the county being lost in the Conflict: "Little Pud" Rabon (son of Pud Rabon from Iron City), Bennie Frank Childree, and Kennith Fields. The Childree man's daddy worked for Hugh Broome as he recalled.

Asking how Alf and Geanette met, I was in for quite a story. The gist of it is they met because Alf's chicken truck and a citrus truck ran together near a poultry dressing plant where she worked in DeFuniak

Springs, Florida. She had to walk about one-third mile up a hill to get to a phone and notify Alf of the accident, a walk she was not so happy about.

Clarence Waddell's son Hubert was a go-between that arranged a double date with the three of them and another young lady from DeFuniak Springs. As it worked out, Alf had the other lady as his date and Hubert was with Geanette. They were essentially thrown together when Hubert walked off from their vehicle with the other lady. As the evening went on, they swapped dates putting Alf and Geanette together for fifty-nine years in June of 2017.

With Alf's father having to spend some time near Cyrene, Georgia, to settle Robert Ingram's estate, Alf took over the reins of Greene Poultry. Robert was married to Lenore, Alf's oldest sister and had died suddenly of a heart attack at the young age of thirty-four.

Curious of how Iron City seemingly lost out to Donalsonville in the first third of the twentieth century, I asked Alf what precipitated the movement of business. He said it was the result of a hard-fought political decision in the Georgia Legislature. A representative from Bainbridge had voted against the formation of Seminole County but was solidly kicked out of office in the next election. Eventually Seminole County was partitioned from Decatur County in 1920. Those supporting it from Seminole County said their decision was ostensibly because of the long distance to Bainbridge to do business.

Looking at the big picture over many years, bad judgment may have been applied over and over throughout the state to create one hundred fifty-nine counties. The costs of the large number of county seats and replication of government services has had to be born subsequently by the Georgia taxpayers. In comparison, Florida has sixty-seven counties.

Once Donalsonville became the county seat, growth and business followed with the city expanding and Iron City shrinking. In a stroke of irony, the Donalsonville city fathers were without money to build a courthouse and borrowed the money from the Iron City government.

Alf told the story of Iron City getting its first teacher. In the late eighteen hundreds, Dr. Jefferson Chason, with his large number of kids, wanted someone to educate them. He brought Alf's grandmother Linnie Campbell Lane to Iron City from Bainbridge to fill the job. She became Iron City's first school teacher when a one-room wooden school building was erected in a location near today's Methodist Church. It burned and a second wood school house was erected on the same lot where the Community Center is today. Alf stated that on June 15, 1931, the second school burned causing the brick school to be constructed which served the Iron City school district's children until its closing in the '60s.

A local character, which I remember, Peg Drake taught at the old school house and eventually became principal. Over the years, Claude Rickman, NP Malcom, Mr. Bentson, Emily Harlow, Ethel Bentley, and Monk Stein are some of those who served in leadership positions at the Iron City schools.

Alf's aunt was instrumental in bringing Malcom to Iron City from Social Circle, Georgia. Alf's grandmother Lane and Malcom became good friends and closely controlled the direction of education for several years and beyond.

Running a boarding house for teachers in the early days of Iron City School, kept Alf's Grandmother Rosa Greene very busy. Alf stated that she boarded several male and female teachers with one bathroom. With a "dug well" and the septic tank only about ten feet apart, God was watching over them to prevent a terrible health problem.

When I asked Alf about what he remembered of Hagan's Still, he had interesting details to share. The still was started by a Mr. Hagan who had a large home adjacent to the operation. Grady Wood McCloud was brought in to manage the production and provided a house at the still. About ten houses were built for the workers and their families which was common practice in those days. In my youth the area was referred to as the Still Quarters. By comparison, textile mills in North Georgia also had built houses, which all had the same floor plan for employees, adjacent to the plants.

To transport the turpentine products, the production crew stored it in large barrels. A side track from the railroad served as parking space for a couple rail cars on which the workers loaded the barrels.

Hagans Still closed in the late thirties per Alf's best memory. The world had changed, and the demand for turpentine had diminished drastically.

Having served as mayor, Alf had many memories of the town's government, political goings-on and its finances. The city's owning the town's only liquor store proved profitable. The first liquor store sat where Tubby and Viola Williams's store was in the '50s and early '60s. After it was torn down, another was built adjacent to the current Cross Hardware which still stands. Larry Batchelor bought it circa 1970, a sale which moved the town out of the liquor business.

For years Seminole County was wet for liquor while surrounding counties were dry, so a large amount of revenue was pumped into Iron City by booze. Alf stated the city had a net worth of roughly $400,000 when he was mayor and still has a hefty amount in the bank. There are no city property taxes and city water costs a flat rate of thirty to forty dollars a month for residents, a bargain. He mentioned a movement from the State of Georgia to place meters on all houses which will drive up the price.

Alf indicated that some of the previous "so-called" leaders in the town could not keep their hands out of the till nor resist manipulating elections. Once they had to find an honest man to run for mayor to clean up the mess. With only three hundred dollars in the city's bank account, someone joked that they should write a check for the paltry amount to clear the decks and start over. On one occasion when Alf was poll manager, he had to garner the support of a group at the polls to physically remove an individual who tried to take over the voting administration in an attempt to allow a preferred candidate to win. As so—can go small town politics—even in Iron City.

Near the end of our conversation, Alf showed me a picture on his wall of JT Lane's store which was located where today's fire department resides. What an interesting picture of a thriving Iron City business in 1898!

Such a pleasant and interesting conversation we had with Alf and Geanette! Yes, he had stories to tell, interesting ones which captured my attention so firmly. He and his wife have had a blessed life. Having moved so many times in my life, I can appreciate the stability of living in the same place for an entire life.

31

Sam Mills, The Mills Family Barnyard

Barnyards

Barnyards hold many memories for people who grew up on a farm. After finding the old Polaroid picture and doing a lot of enlarging and doctoring, I produced the above image. It had importance because it brought back to life precious times.

In the country where I grew up, the barnyards were a center of activity. The picture shows the old barn that Daddy built when I was about six or eight years old, circa 1952. Taken in 1964, the photo shows its deterioration and lack of repair. It had served good purpose in its day but now fell at the mercy of the elements and a "tear-down" decision.

This barn Daddy replaced the one left by Granddaddy Mills which had deteriorated beyond repair. A more traditional, picturesque barn with a hay loft upstairs held loads of charm. Downstairs included animal stalls, storage bins, and an open breezeway. My fondest remembrance, at age six I jumped from the hayloft and landed on the ground to prove I could. At a distance of ten feet, standing in the hay loft was the highest I had been off of the ground.

Barely visible in the picture is the parking place for the C Farmall tractor on the near side of the barn. The old tractor had done its job of helping keep the family fed and housed for about thirteen years and deserved some rest.

In those days if a farmer wanted to change his row spacing for a crop, he had to move the front and back wheels in and out to achieve the correct tracking of the tractor down the rows. It was not an easy, quick process. We had to jack up the tractor's rear end to move the heavy back tires and jack up the front end to re-space the front tires; the process taking the better part of an hour.

The only tractor Daddy owned, he bought circa 1950 and sold it in 1967 for $100. Pulling only two bottom plows, it consumed much gas and time when it was time to "break land" in preparation for the next crop.

Many an hour I spent breaking land with it in January and February freezing and wearing an old army field jacket my brother had given me. Also he had provided me with a pair of army gloves with wool liners which saved fingers; a second pair of pants helped keep the legs warm.

The vertical boards on the far side of the picture gated the stall where the cow spent the night. She was milked before she went into the pen in the afternoon and again when we let her out in the morning. On the ground just outside of the pen, Butterfly and I held many sessions of gathering the milk and developing my handshake.

On the outside edge of the cow stall, water dripped off of the roof and seeped back into the pen where we could dig and harvest plenty of red worms for fishing.

Old Stuff, Newer Stuff, and Stuff

A pig pen was formerly in the back left of the picture in which we would feed pigs when they came out of the pasture. A mud hole and tin shelter gave them relief from the relentless heat in the summers.

This is the same barnyard which Sister, Lloyd, Jerome and I with Mama's supervision had to clean up before we went to see the first movie I remembered. In those days we kept it hoed and "grass clean." When this picture was taken, hoeing had been long given up to the lawn mower. Grass had staked its claim and would never give it up; mowing proved easier than hoeing anyway.

Behind the cow stall stood the mule stall where we kept Clyde the mule until she died when I was about thirteen years old. One of my jobs was to give Clyde a few ears of corn in the late afternoon. Spending the days in a pasture, Clyde's purpose was to farm the garden with Daddy following behind her.

Clyde's passing brought my first experience with the "rendering company." Daddy drove up to Hill Pace's garage and called the rendering man. He came to our farm in a special truck for hauling large, dead animals. With a winch, he moved Clyde into the truck bed. The rendering company was a win/win situation for them and the farmer. Trucking the animal away to make soap or whatever came a lot easier than burying or burning the animal.

To the left in the picture, at the fence by the road was Daddy's gasoline tank which he purchased with about a one hundred fifty gallon capacity after he bought the tractor. It had a hand pump for moving the gas from the tank into vehicles.

In the weeds behind me in the picture are a few pieces of farming equipment which had served their purpose well but now waited for the scrap iron man.

The road behind me going to the top of the hill with a white house is CR 285. About half way to the top of the hill, the current Tom and Brandy Trawick Road exited to the right off of 285.

At the corner of the intersection of the two roads Mama and Daddy had a small "shotgun shack" where they had started their marriage in 1933. The shotgun shack moniker came along because a person could stand on the front porch and fire a shotgun through the house and out the back door without hitting anything. It had about 800 square feet of space and a fully functional "bucket well" in the back yard for water which was still present when I was five or six years old.

If old barnyards could have their say, they would have a lot to share. Pigs were shot and slaughtered. Trailer loads of cotton, corn and peanuts rode through it. Conversations with those who would stop by for a few minutes visit were held. If Mama had an unusual large laundry and the clothesline could not hold it all, she hung the balance on the barnyard fence which was galvanized wire.

Dash and I often played in the barnyard. Building my first rat trap in the barn, I placed a brick high up on a rafter, tied a string to it and tied an ear of corn to the string which suspended it just above the floor. After finishing my Acme, fool-proof, always-catch-'em trap, I calculated the ear of corn was a little too high off of the floor. Without thinking, I pulled on the ear of corn to lower it. Seconds later the brickbat gave me a case of the stars. If I had not been wearing my cowboy hat, I would have needed a trip to see Dr. Baxley to painfully witness his stitching expertise. Wisely I cancelled the rat killing business. Re-design of the trap was not an option after I threw away the drawing board.

The barnyard once belonged to my Granddaddy Mills, so it would have had some harder, more interesting stories to tell of those days. A windmill was there in his time and into the start of my life which I remembered.

Lloyd had once dropped the pump handle adjacent to the windmill on Jerome's toe and severed a piece of it which the doctor sewed back on leaving him with a strange looking toe next to his big one.

In Grandpa Mills day a corn crib sat next to the hog pen. A corn crib of about a twelve by sixteen foot size, had use strictly for corn storage. It survived into the first twelve or so years of my life. One of my early jobs was to obtain corn from it, shuck it, and use a hand corn sheller to shell corn for our chickens.

The barnyard brought a wonderful sight to see at the end of the day since arriving back signaled the end of another day of toil in the fields. Now we only had to deal with the animals, and we could call it a day.

The Boys State T shirt I was wearing in the photo I had received in 1962 when Reuben Roberts, Kennedy Stephens, Glen Hill, Jim Jernigan, Ronald Odom and I were selected to go to Georgia Boys State which was held at a college in College Park, a suburb of Atlanta. We shared the excitement of Sargent Pumphrey taking us in a patrol car. On the way he stopped a car and wrote a warning ticket possibly to demonstrate to us the power of the law. Being the first time I was away from home, separation from my folks did not sit well with me, so the ride back home was highly anticipated.

One of the best parts of getting old, other than being lucky enough to live to enjoy longevity, is the memories. The young have yet to build a memory bank. My brain and my peers' minds are chock full of things from the past which we can enjoy at will.

32

Rolled Over

On a Saturday in the summer of 1962, classmates and I had arrived back from Georgia Boys State held in College Park, Georgia in the afternoon. After settling in and hugging Mama, I asked to use the truck to go down to Buddy Odom's house. With no phone, in-person was the only way I could communicate.

On the way back to our house, I was driving down the now Tom/Brandy Trawick Road at Persimmon Pond which was roughly a quarter mile south of the Brandy Trawick house.

The dirt road in the bottom land area had always been deep sand, especially on the sides where road scrapers routinely pushed the excess sand when scrapping. Being a low place, fresh sand was continually being washed into it increasing the quantity.

Happy to be back home after a week and with my head in the air thinking of everything but staying firmly on the road, I allowed the right front tire to ease into the deep sand on the side of the road. Not going fast, I tried to pull the wheels back into the middle of the road. The sand had a different idea. It simply jerked the wheel further to the right plowing deeper into the sand.

The laws of momentum and physics dictated the weight of the truck had to try to keep going in the straight line it was originally tracking. With the front wheels cut sharply to the right, the truck began to roll over onto its left side. For a second in the crazy slow motion of impending disasters, I prayed it would stop its roll and just flop back onto its wheels upright.

This was not to be as the truck very gently laid over onto its left side. Enough poop had hit my fan to stop the blades dead still.

My first thought was of how disappointed Daddy would be. In our relationship a look of disappointment packed a lot more pow than anger.

What to do? The only way out was to climb up and out of the right side door. As I emerged with my tail firmly tucked between my legs, I began sorting out a plan of action that would hopefully save the day.

Not lying flat on its side, the truck was in a slightly cocked position which gave me an idea of tipping it back on its four wheels. I had seen Superman on TV do similar feats many times. Implementation of the idea proved impossible. After my butt painfully "went out on stem" from straining, Sam decided he was not strong enough or the truck was too heavy, or both.

As anxiety began to set in full force, I saw dust coming up the road, a vehicle. The way my crazy mind worked, I saw the vehicle as a mixed blessing. Was it someone who would tell Daddy? Would they help me out of this jam and keep a secret?

Seeing it was Junior Trawick in a jeep gave me a tremendous sense of relief. Surely he could help me out of this mess, maybe before some other person drove by. Keeping this "under the covers" was my paramount concern.

With a little smile and snicker, Junior said something like, "What happened to you." A stupid question since the scene he saw told it all. My sense of humor was on hiatus.

Quickly explaining my mistake with the sand, he started formulating a solution to my problem. Luckily he had a chain in the jeep, so he hooked it to the truck and rolled it back on its wheels. The chances of my ass staying out of the grinder dramatically improved.

With no obvious damage to the truck, I went to work with a rag wiping off oil which had run out of the engine through the fill spout. My odds of getting out of this unscathed continued to be on the uptick.

No vehicles had passed while we were working, so no relative to squeal to Daddy.

After thanking Junior profusely for virtually saving my life, he drove on toward Brandy's house with me following and staying way clear of the ditches.

Daddy did not learn of my catastrophe until about ten years later when I told him. He had almost nothing to say. A slight smile was his full comment.

33

Tater Bank

Any farm folks ever visit a tater bank to make a withdrawal? Well, you did not need a gun. In my youth we had a tater bank from which we would "withdraw" sweet potatoes for Mama to either bake or slice and fry.

Preserving food was an important issue, so out of necessity in earlier generations the tater bank was invented to store sweet potatoes. It was probably called a bank because at first glance it appeared to be a mound of earth, a bank.

In preparation for the potato harvest, we excavated a shallow hole of diameter dependent on the volume of the quantity of potatoes dug. The hole was lined with pine straw. The potatoes were spaced on the straw in such a manner as to allow air to circulate around them. Sometimes we used teepee stacking to create small spaces between the potatoes.

After the potatoes had been placed, a family member spread a thick layer of pine straw across to cover them. Lastly, the dirt removed from the hole was spread across the top of the pine straw creating a mound or bank.

When Mama said, "Go get us some sweet taters," I knew exactly what she meant. Heading for the tater bank, I dug down into the side of the mound and retrieved as many as she wanted. I pushed some dirt back over the straw and potatoes to continue the preservation.

The potatoes remained well preserved with this practice, and we enjoyed sweet potatoes for months after the harvest.

Tater banking was similar in purpose to smoking meat. In absence of modern refrigeration and super markets, both were methods of preserving food for later consumption.

34

Where to Put Dessert?

After Connie and I married, the first time I wanted to eat dessert on the same plate from which I ate my meal "culture shock" bounded forth from my lovely wife. No way was she ever going to eat dessert on the same plate. It would destroy the taste of the "sweet meats." Coming from a world of routine use of dessert dishes, she should have been amazed.

When I was a kid, Mama had no such thing as dessert dishes. The sweet was eaten on the same plate as the meal. "Clean your plate" was self-motivating. If we did not want turnip juice in our egg custard, we drank the turnip juice. Tilting the plate toward the mouth and drinking vegetable juices was acceptable as normal table manners at our house. If there were bones, they were kicked over to one side of the plate to make room for the dessert.

Napkins, even paper ones, were not bought. That was the purpose the wash bench on the back porch and the shirt sleeve served.

Mama would have not been highly enthusiastic about washing a bunch of dessert dishes by hand anyway. A spoon or knife she supplied in the plate setting only if she thought we needed it.

Those were the days of simple needs and meager provisions. If we had never used dessert dishes, we did not miss them. I wouldn't have missed "not missing the frivolities" for nothing. You can take that to the bank.

Part II Newer Stuff

35

Traveling Man

For a period of ten years during my career, my routine consisted of catching a plane on Monday to go to a project and catching one back home on Friday. Infrequently flights from one project to another had to be taken within a given week which added to the total flights. From 1977 to 1982 we lived in Murfreesboro, Tennessee, and I flew in and out of Nashville. The years of 1982 to 1987 had me commuting into and out of Denver since we lived in Aurora, a suburb of metropolitan Denver.

Being at home with Connie the four nights a week would have greatly been my preference, but the attraction of furthering our financial position in life and focusing on the longer term forced a sacrifice, sucking me into planes, airports and challenging projects. It was an eyes-wide-open tradeoff that I would probably do again, but the inconveniences associated bothered both Connie and me.

On the really bright side, we had at least four honeymoons a month and five in some months. We talked on the phone every night and counted down to the weekend.

Not initially considering traveling to be an adventure, I was amazed looking back at how many things could happen to a person in airports, on planes, and moving from place to place.

Nashville being the country music capital of the world provided a variety of interesting happenings, associated with seeing celebrities. Flying into or out of Nashville about five hundred times presented a number of shoulders to rub and sights to see.

On Friday of the week Elvis died, traveling back from Pauls Valley, OK, I was walking down the concourse in Memphis changing planes and heading to Nashville. As I passed by the outgoing flights screening area, I noticed Linda Thompson, one of Elvis' former girl friends, with a skinny ten or twelve year old blond girl, Elvis' daughter Lisa Marie.

I stopped for a second, got a good look and calculated that Lisa Marie must have been at Elvis' house when he passed and Linda, still a friend of the family, was helping by traveling with Lisa Marie to her mother Priscilla in LA. The solemn looks on their faces communicated the huge loss hanging on their shoulders.

Having accumulated a quantity of frequent flyer miles circa 1986 Connie and I were treating ourselves to a Maui trip and were flying out of Denver. Shooting the works, I had converted enough miles to obtain first class tickets. As it was, we had to take a late night flight out of Denver which was stopping at Los Angeles for a plane change on the way to Maui.

Boarding the plane early, we had settled in our seats with glasses of champagne ready to enjoy, enjoy, enjoy. As luck would have it, another sighting of celebrities occurred. The LA Lakers had played the Denver Nuggets in Denver earlier that night, so all of a sudden this army of giants, dressed in warmup suits, came walking into our area and sat all around us.

Being not of a nature to push ourselves onto celebrities, we enjoyed our champagne and observed.

With no history of being an avid basketball fan, I recognized only two players: Kareem Abdul-Jabbar and Magic Johnson.

The guys could not be mistaken for a bundle of excitement. Every player got comfortable in his seat, pulled an airline blanket over his head, and went to sleep. The strenuous game had taken something out of them, and they wanted to go to sleep for the approximately two hour flight to Los Angeles.

Departing with the gang at Los Angeles, we ended up at the plane exit door standing next to Kareem. Feeling as diminutive as I had been in my life, he stood about a foot taller and possessed the largest hands I had seen in my life—easily twice my size.

Always on the lookout for the supposed "upper crust," the celebrity I saw most frequently out of Nashville was Minnie Pearl, known off the stage as Mrs. Henry Cannon. About three times she was on her way out of Nashville on Monday morning presumably on her way to a personal appearance.

She came off as a friendly sort with people coming up to say hello often. Mrs. Cannon would wear a business suit with her hair in a ball on the back of her head and curls in front, a huge contrast to the Minnie Pearl on the Grand Ol Opry.

As many times as I went through screening, something unfortunate had to happen one day and it did. Travelers who have flown in that period know the routine of the airport screening. Take off your belt, watch, and pocket change and deposit them in a small container which would flow through the X-ray machine. If anything was being carried, it had to go on the conveyor and through the screener. Routinely carrying a briefcase, I tossed it on the conveyor along with the other items.

After walking to the other side, the screener scanned me with one of the hand held device, which distracted me momentarily. I then grabbed all of my items and the briefcase off of the end of the conveyor and headed for my plane.

When I got to the facility where I was going to work that week, I opened my briefcase and saw unfamiliar possessions, not mine. My heart missed a couple of beats knowing my entire work life was in my briefcase. A huge problem deposited itself in my lap. Quickly I figured that another guy and I switched briefcases accidentally at the screening conveyor.

Immediately I found a phone and called American Airlines to report my situation and ask for help getting the cases switched back. They were helpful and assured me the other guy would be calling. Later in the day I received a call, and they gave me a flight number into Waco, Texas, on which my briefcase would arrive. What a relief! Came out of that one intact with all my nerves, though frayed.

Being a frequent flyer, American Airlines would occasionally offer me a first class upgrade to travel back home. On Friday afternoon after a hard week, I welcomed the "endless bottle of wine" in first class.

On this day after settling into my seat, I noticed a familiar face, Tony Orlando. He was a couple rows forward on the front seat in first class, a ball of energy and personality. This occurred around the mid-eighties, so Tony had already left Dawn and the "Tie a Ribbon Around the Old Oak Tree" money was getting moldy in the bank. Tony had added considerable girth and was almost constantly on his feet talking to the female flight attendant or the passengers on the front row. I had to wonder if he was on "uppers."

One afternoon I was on a flight that had to stop in Las Vegas, so the passengers were given maybe twenty minutes to get off the plane and stretch their legs. On a lark I decided to play the slot machines which were a few feet beyond the screening area.

Cashing a couple dollars for eight quarters, I was ready to break the bank quickly and get back on my flight. Swapping quarters with the machine for about ten minutes, all of a sudden this alarm goes off and one hundred quarters came tumbling into the tray.

A hundred quarters has weight and volume. How was I going to get them quickly through the screener and onto the plane? My solution was to put half in each of my sport coat pockets. I waddled over to the screening area, removed my coat and sent it through the screening conveyor. Retrieving the coins and coat on the other side, I awkwardly raced for the plane.

It was lucky for Vegas that I only had a few minutes. With more time I may have had to leave the premises under complimentary armed guard.

A portion of the time I flew out of Nashville, a black guy, junior engineer named Wallace Lipscomb traveled with me. Unbelievably Wallace appeared a carbon copy of Sherman Hemsley who played George Jefferson on the Jeffersons TV series.

Usually it would happen on a plane. A person would walk by and gawk at Wallace. Occasionally one would ask if he were George Jefferson. Gracefully he would deny the accusation, but intruders persisted and did not want to believe him. They thought he did not want to be noticed. I asked him whether he had considered selling his autograph.

One day Wallace and I were strutting through the Nashville Airport and Wallace exclaimed, "There's ol' Fist Full of Dollars." Looking in the direction he was pointing, I confirmed that it was Clint Eastwood wearing Wrangler jeans with pullover and with him Sandra Locke.

During the time of their relationship, they appeared together for a number of years making five or more movies. Her parents lived in Shelbyville, Tennessee, so apparently they had been visiting her folks and were on the way back to Los Angeles.

Flying back home from St. Louis, my company's home office, it was Friday and I was headed for Nashville and my baby's arms. I had a drink or two and fell asleep on the flight, a rare occurrence.

Awakening, the plane was taxiing up to the ramp for debarking of the passengers. Quickly I grabbed my briefcase from the overhead and headed for the door with the other travelers.

Feeling a need for a trip to a restroom, I spotted one and entered. As I was standing there doing my business, I saw this advertisement on the wall promoting an event coming to Cincinnati. Cincinnati! I am not in Nashville! The plane will be leaving going onto Nashville, and I am not on it.

With a wet pants leg, I ran down the concourse at full speed and got on the plane as they were closing the door. What a freakout moment that was! I etched a brain note to myself: "When you take a nap on the plane, know which city you are in when it stops."

With extensive traveling in the '80s, missing Donnie and Marie would have been difficult. As I was waiting for my suitcase at baggage claim after arriving at Santa Anna, California, I noticed the familiar face of Donnie Osmond traveling with no entourage. He was there alone to receive his bag and pull it to the parking lot. He seemed so serious and preoccupied with no smiles for anyone.

On a Friday afternoon, trekking down the concourse in Dallas, I noticed this pretty little lady, none other than Marie Osmond, coming straight at me with a following of at least ten people. She was five feet five inches tall, but the taller people with her made her appear smaller. She was picking them up and laying them down at top speed. My guess was that she was hustling to a connecting flight. With the entourage along a concert must have been in the offing that night.

In Waco, Texas, something occurred which I had never thought would happen. When I went to work at the facility that morning, I fully expected to stay another night and work there the next day. A phone call interrupted those plans creating a need for me to leave that day and go to another destination.

When the time came, I drove to the airport in Dallas to catch a flight. As I turned in the rental car, I found no suitcase in the trunk to take to baggage check-in. My suitcase with all my belongings strewn around the room resided at a motel in Waco.

Having stayed many times at the Holiday Inn, I called the desk and told them what had happened. They agreed to throw my stuff in the suitcase and save it at the desk until I arrived the next week. What a relief!

In the future when my plans changed during a given day, I carefully considered the details that must be covered to avoid creating a problem.

In the middle eighties, Friday afternoon found me boarding a plane in Los Angeles. Having taken my seat in coach, I heard this noisy group coming down the aisle. Leading the pack was Ray Stevens, country music star. He was babbling and laughing saying, "I got a bullet." Not being studied in music business jargon, I was hoping he did not have a gun to go with it. He took a seat a couple rows behind me and across the aisle.

Later research revealed that he had a hot song that was on the way up the charts, a bullet. The group had attended the Country Music Awards the night before and were still hyped and excited.

The only other person I recognized was Dottie West, who was accompanied by a much younger husband or companion. They sat five or six rows in front of me and were more sedate than Ray.

On another flight, by the window, one row ahead of me on my side of the plane sat a long-dark-haired Bobbie Gentry of "Ode to Billie Joe" fame. What a treat that was! She was gorgeously beautiful, quiet, and traveling alone.

One of the biggest strokes of luck Connie and I had came when she visited me in Santa Anna, California while I was on a project. We decided to eat at this popular restaurant and were lucky to get seats, acknowledging the packed parking lot.

After enjoying our meal, we were told by the waitress we could join other patrons in a huge bar room for a concert. Not knowing who was appearing, we wandered into the packed room and lo and behold there was David Frizzell and Shelly West. Not long after their so-hot hit "On Broadway" had been released, we heard them sing the song among their other many hits. Shelly was an unbelievable knockout in a leather pants/vest top outfit. Such a pleasant surprise: free made it better.

Flying into or out of Denver about five hundred times invited an opportunity for at least one case of in-air trouble; it came in scary fashion. Friday on a hot summer afternoon had me on a flight getting close to the airport.

The pilot came on the speaker to inform us heavy thunderstorms and hail were disrupting air traffic. He indicated we would need to go into a holding pattern and circle the airport waiting for landing instructions.

It seemed routine until the fierce air currents common to Denver started giving the plane a few hostile bounces. In a few minutes hostile turned into ferocious and nerve endings ruptured. It seemed like the plane was dropping a hundred feet then rising a similar amount.

Then I smelled it and saw it. People were reaching for barf bags and depositing yesterday's lunch. The sound of the coughing and gagging accompanied by the putrid smell caused others to reach for barf bags. It became self-perpetuating: the more people tossed up, the more they recruited new participants in the projectile-vomiting contest.

I sat there with all my food neatly tucked inside and gasped at what was going on. The attendants were stumbling up and down the aisles to help people and to hold infants while mothers tossed up.

Was there a way for this to end? I wanted so badly to be on the ground but not in a burning pile.

After about thirty minutes, the plane landed. The cleanup crew was going to find an unwelcome surprise. Gas masks and rubber gloves would have been good tools to have.

Catching another flight to LA, I noticed a very familiar face, Red Skelton, who boarded and sat in first class. This raucous, unhinged comic sat in silence. When he spoke to a flight attendant, he used few words but was very polite. Possibly he had done a standup concert the night before and was on his way back home.

Having watched this funnyman so often in the fifties, sixties, and seventies, this was a special treat. What a career he had!

Departing Little Rock on a Friday afternoon, I had taken my seat and noticed a familiar face walking into first class, Jerry Clower. As Red Skelton, he was somber as a funeral director. He stowed his small bag in the overhead, took his seat, and said nothing unless spoken to. These guys have to be "in character" so much we can guess they take a quiet break when the opportunity arrives.

A fellow traveler asked me if I had visited the Crown Room in Dallas. Having not experienced the pleasure, I asked him to tell me about it. He related that it was sponsored by American Airlines, and it was for the enjoyment of frequent fliers. He suggested that the next time I had extra time between flights in Dallas, I should ask any AA employee the location of the Crown Room.

Eventually finding the opportunity to locate this special refuge, I was in for a welcome surprise. It was a luxuriously furnished respite for frequent fliers which offered free booze, beer, wine and snacks on an all-you-can-stumble-out-the-door-with basis. Could I be dreaming? What a deal!

A company I worked for had an apartment in NY City which was used by merchandising personnel and could be requisitioned by others if it were available. To go on vacation in Barbados, Connie and I had to depart from NY, so I secured the place for an overnight stay.

Having not visited New York, I was somewhat excited by the occasion. The ride from the airport was shock number one. The taxi driver zipped in and out of traffic like he was in a car race. At times with breakneck speed, inches separated us from a collision or a side-swipe; I realized we had to take one back to the airport the next day.

Old Stuff, Newer Stuff, and Stuff

A couple of heavy suitcases we had stored in the trunk of the cab. When we arrived at our building, I noticed the driver stood back and allowed me to retrieve them from storage. Being a little amazed at his rudeness, I got rude, too. I handed him two quarters, and Connie and I started making our way to our apartment for the night. As we got to the other side of the street, he threw the quarters in our direction, said something unintelligible, and jumped in his car. I had heard stories of New York's ungraciousness, now I had lived one.

The people such as those in sales who spend an entire career flying around the country or world have my respect. Ten years of punishment filled my stomach with air travel. The time spent in airports waiting for a plane are the longest minutes I have spent anywhere.

The airlines temporarily lost my bag six or eight times, but in those days they delivered it to your destination when it was located. Not one bag was permanently lost. A few times a courier delivered a suitcase to our home on Saturday.

The travelers who tried to put an oversize bag into the overhead storage would thoroughly grind my grits. Other passengers had to witness the pushing and pounding trying to get ten pounds of crap in a five pound bag followed by an argument with a flight attendant. Uncommonly the plane had a slight delay while the attendant took a "won't-fit" bag to have it checked for storage in the cargo hold.

When again I was able to be home every night with Connie, I appreciated home and her even more. Being one of the homebodies, "On The Road Again" had no appeal for Sam.

36

Windjammer Barefoot Cruise

In circa 1984 at roughly the ages of forty, in our prime fun time years, I noticed an ad in a magazine for Windjammer Barefoot Cruises. Reading the sales pitch, I became intrigued with the adventure, the beauty, the romance, and fun of a cruise on a wooden sailing ship which toured five islands in the Caribbean.

Three or four wooden sailing ships in their fleet offered cruises which sailed to various islands of the West Indies. The one that caught my eye started at Saint Martin and went to Nevis, Montserrat, Saint Barts and Antiqua with passengers waking each morning at a different island. The more I read, the more I considered the possibility.

Taking the magazine home to Connie, she was equally inspired and ready to pack bags. I got busy picking dates around my job schedule and making reservations through the Windjammer booking office out of Miami.

Being on a project near Dallas, I asked Connie to fly from Denver to Dallas from which we would together take our first leg of the trip. An overnight stay in Dallas took us to Neiman Marcus. Having never entered such a high class store, we thought it would be interesting to walk through and check price tags. We both bought something but I can only remember mine, an outrageously expensive fifty-four dollar beach hat. When I saw the beauty hanging on a hat rack, it said out load, "I'm for Sam."

The next morning we departed for Miami and on to St Martin where we had to spend a night in a hotel for embarkation the next morning. St Martin is half Dutch and half French. What a strange situation for two governments to be managing an island! The area had an American stamp on it with well-known fast food restaurants visible everywhere.

Up early the next morning, we were eager to board the ship with about one hundred-thirty passengers and forty crew members. It was truly an old time, rustic wooden sailing ship with lots of mahogany. It reminded me of pirate ships I had seen in Errol Flynn movies but with much better accommodations. We liked about everything: the food, our room, the dining room, the bar, the captain and the friendly crew. The only serious drawback was cold showers. Talking about a fast shower, it did not take long in that water.

The first day we spent sailing to Nevis, the birthplace of Alexander Hamilton, and getting to know our fellow travelers. It rained all day, so a crowd stood around the bar in swimsuits, drinking and enjoying a jovial time. They had any beer you wanted as long as you wanted a Heineken. A variety of mixed drinks and wine complimented the remainder of the offering.

As joke telling began, I realized that my large repertoire of redneck jokes would be unheard by my new buddies, so I gave them a good dousing in Southern humor. We had people from far flung parts of the US: New York, LA, Dallas and many places in between. We spent several hours around the bar telling jokes, being rained on, and splashed by waves coming over the side of the ship at times.

Each morning after breakfast, we boarded a launch to the island where we had arrived during the night before. We spent the day touring the shops and sampled the local cuisine for lunch. The food on Nevis and Monserrat did not impress us, but St Barts had a different food story to tell.

A modern French Island, St Barts amazed everyone. The beauty of the yachts in the harbor and the city nestled along the sides of a mountain exceeded picture-postcard pretty. The people and the community made us feel like being in French Americana.

Our gang of fifteen or twenty went to lunch at a nice restaurant up on the side of the mountain overlooking the beach. Whatever type of baked fish we had, it tasted totally delicious and a wine offering of pouilly fuisse had us calling for more. Slightly inebriated, not versed in the French language, and with diminished judgment, I bought a couple bottles for the table. Including food, our bill came to one hundred twenty dollars. Unable to correctly exchange the value of francs into dollars delivered me a much large bill than I had anticipated. My charge card groaned and waggled with it, and I paid the largest tab of my life until that point.

Back down the mountain to the beach, it only took a glimpse to notice that it was a topless beach. Everything I saw was in two's. The French had few inhibitions compared to this old laid back South Georgian. Eye strain was a common complaint among us travelers.

We spent the afternoons back on the ship lounging on the deck with friends. Four girls in their twenties from New York and a couple from LA, roughly our ages, came to be our hangout group. All of the girls were in college, loads of fun and mature for their ages. Being in college and affording the expensive cruise told me someone's parents were loaded.

The longer we lounged, the rowdier we got, so by the evening meal we were well cranked up. Connie and I enjoyed ourselves immensely. Not far past dinner we would be headed to bed to dream of the cold shower in the morning.

About age forty the most unusual man I met had booked solo trips on all the Windjammer ships and was going to spend most of the summer sailing. He must have been independently rich but traveled with only what he carried in a large backpack.

The captain had a standing rule that anyone up at 6:00 a.m. received free Bloody Mary's. Needless to say not many, if any, people took advantage of the offer, certainly not us.

Antigua had the most persistent cab drivers experienced on the trip. They harassed us from the shore to downtown begging us to ride. We understood it was their lives and livelihood, but we needed the exercise. Antigua did not have much to offer, so we soon returned to the ship after lunch.

Looking back on our lives, a number of things are not candidates for do-over. We liked the Windjammer Cruise so well that if we could magically do that number again, we would not hesitate. The only thing different we would do is take along a couple of friends to add to the sharing of the adventure.

37

Close Call

Having happened so long ago, I had almost forgotten this unfortunate happening. So many times the Good Lord's angel has been riding on our shoulders and circa 1975 His protection made a huge difference for Connie and I.

My boss wanted me to help at one of the company's plants near Livingston, Tennessee, so Connie and I temporarily lived there for a few weeks.

Not being a highly populated area, we confronted a shortage of motel rooms. No rooms were available within a suitable distance, so we rented a mobile home and traveled back to our residence in LaFollette, Tennessee, every weekend.

The furnishings of this "Ritz Carlton" mobile home were sparse and reminded me of that old song "Bare Necessities."

The television in the living room was adequate except Connie and I liked to watch our programs while reclining. Taxing our creativity, we pulled the mattress from the bedroom onto the living room floor.

Awakened about four in the morning, we heard unusually magnified thunder and lightning. Thinking another heavy thunderstorm, I was the picture of cool until the wind started blowing harder with a sound similar to the "tornado freight train," and huge water droplets began hitting the side of the trailer like machine gun bullets. With these sounds being unlike any I had experienced, I told Connie that we should get under the mattress quickly. She crawled under her side and I mine, and we met in the middle, cowering with fear.

The trailer started shaking and moving as I started asking our Maker to spare us for another day. The whole experience lasted five minutes or less but seemed much longer.

Then it stopped other than continuing heavy rain hitting the windows and roof. We had no power nor water. What had happened?

We heard the sound of sirens from an emergency vehicle on the way to help someone. Aware that there could be downed power lines, we stayed inside and peeped out the windows.

Activity and flashing lights next door grabbed our attention. A trailer had been turned on its side, and firemen were trying to extricate someone from the dwelling. The occupants, an older couple, had been saved by providence and were only shaken up.

As daylight emerged, I opened the trailer door, and to my amazement the steps anchored in concrete were about three feet from the structure. Now my world was really rocked. The twister, or whatever it was, had moved our trailer.

The Old Master had saved us from harm as He would several times. I often wondered if He had to put on an extra shift of angels to watch over us since fate had been tempted too many times in our lives. Thanks so much for a loving Lord.

38

Sometimes the Best Intentions

Several lady guests were at our house for lunch, and they had a pressing question as they came through the front door, "Why do you have three satellite dishes?" It was a fair question because most yards have one satellite dish. "We had to be different," I retorted.

Quickly I told them that one was for Dish TV, one for Dish internet and one was a mistake by the beloved Dish technicians. Only two were functional and one was defunct. As I spoke, I deposited a brain note to remove the unused one.

A mental question popped into my mind, "Of all the people that have been to our house in the last three years, how did these ladies decide to become inquisitive about my number of satellite dishes today?" I should have smelled a "karma rat" at this point but was oblivious.

Shortly after we moved back to Seminole County in 2013, I worked on securing TV and internet reception. After an aborted relationship with Direct TV followed by their collection agency repetitively sending me a bill for $400 + as their costs of setting up their system, I settled on Dish as the better of two evils.

After meeting every satellite technician Dish had in the area and learning "all of their children and all of their names" from the Roger Miller song, they finally located a dish in our front yard which would receive a good signal for TV and another dish for internet. It was the fifth technician, a trainer, who held the charm.

After these many trips, I ended up with an extra satellite dish in the yard. The internet dish and the non functional satellite dish were side by side. The functioning TV dish was thirty feet away.

Having had the item, "Remove satellite dish" on my do list for a couple weeks, I decided that the perfect time to complete a productive task had arrived. The extra dish partially restricted mowing in the area, so I saw the undertaking as a big plus which would not take much time.

As "Fix-it Sam" knows, small projects start out in the mind as simple and quick, but the element of surprise reserves the right to pop out like an evil spook to turn it into an all-nighter.

Retrieving my zip saw with the blade that cuts metal, I headed to the satellite dish which should be removed. Observing the internet dish and the unused satellite dish side by side, I compared each to the functioning TV dish. One of the two was the same size as the dish-in-use, so I assumed it must be the defunct TV dish, the other being the internet dish which was much smaller.

As I set about cutting the pole close to the ground, little did I know "trouble" was circling my block looking for a parking place to create havoc. In a couple of minutes, the pole was cut loose and gently placed against the house for later disposal.

Feeling proud of how well and how quickly I had dispatched the bothering dish, I put my tool away and went back inside for a little Facebook interaction.

As I clicked on the internet site and waited, I noticed that it was loading slowly, in fact, not at all. It is not unusual to have to do a reset by unplugging the dish modem and restarting my laptop, so I did. Still no internet. I reset it again. No luck.

Now I began connecting event A, removing the TV dish, with event B, no internet. Suspicions were strong that I had created my own trouble, the worst kind. I had diddled in my own nest.

I called Dish and after a few minutes on hold, I connected with this nice technician that checked his instruments to see if I had service. He told me that my service had gone down an hour and twenty minutes ago. In my psychic brilliance, I told him t I suspected why service was lost.

After describing the dish I had removed, he assured me I had taken down the internet dish. My heart sank to my big toenail on my left foot.

He scheduled a "trusted" Dish technician to re-connect my internet dish. Having my iPhone for backup, I took comfort that life would go on.

I had the six dollars per month insurance charge for Dish covering any tech calls. If the technician tried to dump a huge bill on my plate, I was going to tell him the importance of technicians cleaning up their messes as they go. If they had removed the unused dish, all in Camelot would have been peachy keen.

Assuring myself this was by far my most "brilliant move of the year," I took great satisfaction that there were only three days left in 2016. New projects I immediately cancelled for the rest of the year to prevent surpassing this doozie. Looking forward to 2017 and more unwanted surprises, I pray that they are no worse than cutting down the wrong satellite dish.

The Dish technician came and left the house with mission accomplished and no charges. He removed the nonfunctional dish from its pole and mounted the internet dish back on the same pole. The wounds were healed for the satellite internet but not for my ego which had open festers.

Ironically a few days later I received an ad in the mail offering high speed Windstream DSL internet service at our address. Well, wasn't that grand! I had just re-erected a dish that I would soon not need. If high speed DSL had been available in 2013, I would have gotten it rather than Dish internet. Dish gives you a limited amount of data at a higher cost. Windstream DSL offers unlimited data at $20 per month cheaper.

So I went with Windstream and got busy cutting down the satellite dish pole which had been re-setup two weeks before. If anyone needs a satellite dish removed, let me know. I am getting really good at it.

39

The Travails of Being a "Mister Chef"

With some guests coming, I had decided to make two pecan pies and potato salad. Checking a carton in the fridge, I counted nine eggs. I could not remember when those had been bought but was sure it was in Oshiferbrains's second disastrous administration. My mind had been blocking out a lot of stuff from that debacle.

With not enough eggs to make both items, I fetched another carton from Wally World.

Since childhood, it remains about impossible for me to throw away food. Food's preciousness in those days inhibits me from overcoming the imprint in my feeble brain. The "Manchurian Candidate of food" has been programmed to never waste.

Making the two pecan pies first, I cracked the older eggs and deposited them into the mixing bowl which came with my blender. After adding the other ingredients and cranking up the mixer, I observed there were globules of the eggs which kept floating through the mixer blades and not breaking down. It was time to turn up the speed on the mixer, but the lumps did not disappear completely; they got smaller.

The pecan pies were delicious and our guests did not complain, at least not openly at the table. A couple of small dark spots on top revealed where a few globules burned. Perhaps not the best solution but old eggs can work with pecan pies I concluded.

To make potato salad I placed eggs in a pan of water to boil. As they started boiling, I noticed the two eggs with "Eggland's Best" stamped on the end (the older ones) did not sink like the newer ones. Instead they floated with the small end up. I guessed they wanted to boil differently from the others.

After boiling, I cooled, peeled and sliced them into the potato salad mix. After thoroughly mixing the potato salad with all ingredients, I gave it a much anticipated taste and found it delicious; Connie agreed.

What did I learn? Old eggs can be used in a kitchen. We did not throw away food when I was a kid, and I can't get over it without extended counseling. Everything worked out fine. Out of conservatism, in the future I think I will boil eggs before they get old and have them as a snack if a recipe doesn't need them.

40

God Acts in Mysterious Ways

In April of 2016, we started the wheels turning to get Connie into another clinical trial testing an experimental Alzheimer's drug. My research indicated that a medicine called Bryostatin I was being studied by two clinics in Atlanta. The drug had been successfully tested on mice and on at least one person with dramatic results.

After calling the clinic, Connie and I drove to Atlanta for a conference to learn more about joining the trial. The only obstacle the screener and doctor identified at the time was the fact that Connie had received a last IV of monoclonal antibodies on February 1, 2016, at the end of another clinical trial. They stated the necessity for a one-year waiting period before a person who received monoclonal antibodies could be included in the study. The doctor who owns the clinic stated they would seek a six-month waiver meaning we could join the study approximately August 1, 2016.

In May I received a call from the screener who informed us they had received the waiver, and the understanding was they would strive for our formal screening in late July with a start in the study around August 1.

Finally we received a call about August 12 and went to Atlanta for the screening. The screening went fine with us spending five hours in interviews and testing. Everything seemed on track.

About a week later, I received a call from the screener with a question about Connie's meds. He noted that she was getting a med for seizures, so I gave him the whole story of the seizures which started in the fall of 2015. The neurologist managing the clinical trial we were in at the time had diagnosed the attacks based on my descriptions of what Connie had experienced.

At the time I mentioned that Connie has chronic lymphocytic leukemia which our oncologist said will not affect her life span. It is in zero stage at this point with no medication being given. Meds will be prescribed when the doctor sees any progression of the disease.

Expecting an answer soon, I sent two emails to the screener and left a phone message for his assistant a few days later asking for a disposition. After getting no answer for two weeks, I wrote a letter to the doctor who owns the clinic.

He called me and apologized for what had happened. Our application should not have been held up. The problem being the screener felt his responsibility was finished when he last talked to us, and the clinic coordinator was supposed to be handling our application from that point. As I delved deeper into it, I developed a strong impression the screener was trying to throw the coordinator under the bus for an unknown reason. He could have easily sent me an email explaining I should communicate with the coordinator.

A day or two later the coordinator called and apologized. She had more questions about the chronic leukemia. Our oncologist had already written a letter to them stating that it was permissible for her to be in the study with her diagnosis. The coordinator asked for another letter with a more detailed answer, which was only splitting hairs, stating permission for Connie to be in the study. The oncologist essentially wrote the same letter again.

Around the end of September, I received an email from the other clinic we had considered for the clinical trial stating the study was about to be closed to any more participants. Alarmed I called the doctor, and he said they would try to get us under the wire, but we had to be screened again since it had been too long since the first screening, hugely disappointing news.

We drove to Atlanta for a second screening. Everything seemed to go well, but the doctor told us he could make no promises on getting Connie into the study.

A few days later the doctor called me and said there were two problems from the drug company sponsor of the clinical trial: The presence of seizures was unacceptable, and anyone with chronic leukemia had to be diagnosed for at least two years prior to joining the study.

At this point I told the doctor, "That is the way God wanted it." He apologized again for the poor handling of our application and stated they would look for other studies in which Connie may participate.

Ironically we had been working on the seizure problem, but I saw that the chronic leukemia requirement was insurmountable.

In early October 2016, God set me to thinking really hard about the seizures. I am the only one who had witnessed them. Having described them to the neurologist in the previous clinical trial, he immediately diagnosed seizures and prescribed a medicine back in October 2015. The "seizures" continued at random times accumulating a total of about five. All had the same characteristics. Connie would pass out or almost pass out for a very brief period, under thirty-seconds.

Discussing the problem with my cousin who is an RN, we decided that there was a strong chance it was blood pressure or heart-related. I made an appointment with my cardiologist for Connie who had never seen one because she has always had a healthy heart. She has high blood pressure, which her 93 year-old mother has had for thirty years plus, but very treatable.

Seeing Dr. Miles and describing the "seizures," he immediately said it very probably was BP related. It was definitely not seizures. He asked about Connie's water consumption. Coffee and tea do not count as water intake, so she had been getting about half of water needed per his opinion. He said that I should ensure she gets fifty ounces a day. He discontinued one of her blood pressure meds, Amlodipin and told her to keep taking Losartan,

To be thorough, he ordered an echocardiogram and a stress test. We would have results on those November 22 when he would probably discontinue the seizure medicine.

What I learned from this is that second and even third opinions should be sought when health diagnoses are serious. Two neurologists, the clinical neurologist and a neurologist in Dothan, had diagnosed seizures. Our family physician had not questioned the diagnosis. It took God to lead me to what appeared to be the right place.

The cardio doctor's recommendations did not bear fruit. The fainting got worse. As God would have it, my cousin Janet Ausley Carver searched on the internet and learned one of Connie's long-time Alzheimer medicines could be causing the fainting. She fainted three times the week before January 6 when we discontinued the med which she could do without. No more fainting has occurred after January 6.

Our present neurologist said there was a five percent chance that long term usage of Aricept will cause fainting.

As of April, 2017, about seventy-five Alzheimer's drugs are moving through the research and development pipeline. We pray that one of these drugs will knock a home run in the next year or so. God has given us time. Every day I thank Him for His love and grace. The war is never over until He indicates it is.

41

Anatomy of a Scam

Having spent thirty years working with PC's, laptops and notebook computers, it would appear that I would know better. Crooked people populate the internet who love to do harm to others for financial gain. When I let my guard down for a fleeting second, trouble climbed into my wagon.

On April 14, 2016, I was using my notebook computer, when an ad for MacKeeper popped up on my screen offering antivirus protection and other software solutions.

They chose their product name wisely to seemingly offer some promise of an Apple-related product. Since buying my MacBook Air, I had several Apple offers pop up on my screen which I denied.

I wondered why Apple had not offered me an antivirus protection before and decided that this was it. I clicked on the ad, paid with my credit card and downloaded it.

A few minutes later I noticed that my computer had gotten extraordinarily slow. A screen popped up with a number to call to fix a computer problem. I decided to call it and got a guy who wanted ninety-nine dollars to fix my computer problem. I smelled a very large, stinking rat. How did he know that I had a problem? I declined his help and decided to fix the problem with my knowledge.

A virus had no doubt been deposited in my computer. My first thought was to kill off MacKeeper. Solving the problem was not going to be so easy since the virus had already set up a trojan program in my computer which stood alone from MacKeeper.

Frustrated, I decided to download a trial version of Norton Antivirus. Norton confirmed the presence of two viruses and eliminated them, so to speak.

A while later I noticed my slow problem continued. I ran Norton's scan of my computer again, and it found the same virus. Furrowing of my brow became deep ditches on my forehead. Now what do I do?

After reading up on MacBooks "system restore," I decided the only way to dispose of the virus was to restore which effectively downloaded a new version of the Apple OS software. I was amazed at its superiority to the similar Windows restore. It replaced my operating system and left all my files intact. Wow! The virus was gone.

I am told that antivirus software with Mac products is unnecessary. I view the proposition with a jaundiced eye having experienced such a frustrating problem. The only rationale I saw was to buy the disc if possible when adding an application, and avoid downloading from the internet unless it is Apple's store site.

Realizing how well Mac's restore worked, perhaps I would not buy the Norton antivirus when my trial period ended. I could use good judgement, avoid problem sites and use restore if I get snookered again.

They had billed my credit card $118.80 for MacKeeper, so I filed a disputed charge claim with American Express. I finally called PayPro Global who handled the charge, and they removed the entry from my credit card charges.

I googled MacKeeper and found they are notorious for malware, which dumps viruses into computers. Why there is not any action by the FCC to control these problems amazes me.

An unappreciated grand opportunity for life to take the boredom out of life had landed in my lap, but I dumped it back in the gutter where it belonged.

42

Plumbing for Dollars

Being of a conservative nature and refusing to pay someone to do for which I am trained, I decided to replace the faucets and drains in our master bath. When we remodeled four bathrooms in our Florida home about ten years ago, I learned painfully well how to install faucets. The school of hard knocks graduated a somewhat adept weekend plumber.

Saturday afternoon I chose to begin and opened the box containing the faucets. Mistake number one, I ordered only one set of faucets. Absent minded, half-cracked Sam could only do half of the project. My nerves began to tatter prematurely; the worst was yet to come.

Immediately, I logged on the internet and ordered another identical set before, with my luck, they were discontinued. They would arrive the next week.

To save fourteen trips to the utility room for additional tools, I brought most of my tools into the bathroom. The instructions displayed pictures of a wrench and a screwdriver as the only tools needed. What a sense of humor they must have!

After deciding to attack the spout first since it appeared to be the hardest to remove, I dove into the project. The nut holding the spout in place was on the underside of the countertop and nestled behind the concavity of the sink, provided about enough room for a small monkey or a dwarf to work, but somehow I crunched my old bones and gained limited access.

Having purchased a "wrench on a stick," a plumber's tool for accessing nuts in tight spaces, a few years back, I was convinced that I could loosen the nut. In a contorted position with most of my upper body under the countertop, I plundered around in the area of the nut with the tool.

Visibility was limited even with a flashlight. Convinced that I had gotten a grasp of something with the wrench, I began turning what I thought was the nut. After a few turns, I strained to take a glimpse of what I was turning. Grabbing the flashlight for an affirming look, I discovered that I had been twisting the pipe on which the nut was threaded; therefore damaging the threads the nut needed to turn on to be removed. The nut coming off from the bottom was not going to happen. The plot thickened causing me to mumble unmerciful and unintelligible oaths.

Deciding to cut off the spout to allow pushing of the nut and pipe through to the bottom of the counter, I chose as my next approach. My zip saw is a tool I had not brought from the utility room, so I retrieved it. It carries the name zip saw because with a couple of zips your fingers can end up on the floor still wiggling. Great care must be applied in its use or it's off to the emergency room with fingers on ice in a plastic bag.

Making four or five cuts on the spout, this cloud of metal dust hovered in the bath and settled over the countertop, floor and commode. Looked like "clean-up" would require a little longer than planned.

I finally removed the spout and pushed the pipe and nut loose from the top of the counter causing it to fall to the space below. What relief! Two hours into the project things were going really well. I had removed the spout. "Plumber excellente" had performed a textbook "spoutus removus," the scientific term for the operation.

I attacked the faucets dealing with the similar problems of tight space by extending my body into positions not intended by nature and probably illegal in some states. I spent another hour and a half removing them.

Connie came into the bath to check on me. She wanted to know if there was anything she could do to help. I requested two things: a glass of water and extensive prayers.

Last, I removed the drain pipe from the bottom of the sink which was the easiest task of all.

Old Sam was tired and his nerves were in need of repair, so I cancelled the project for the rest of the day for recovery. With a good night's sleep, the task will appear smaller tomorrow. Yeah! Right!

All of Sunday afternoon I spent installing the two faucets and spout. Again, accessing the nuts to turn in tight spaces and twisting my upper body into stressful positions took its toll and lots of time. The sore muscles made me feel like finding a rocking chair and a shawl.

The next morning I installed the drain, the easy work. I already knew that I had no water leaks since I turned on the water to the faucets the previous afternoon; with no unexpected water leaks, happy days were in my midst again.

Considering the massive flow of stomach acid and "talking in strange tongues" with half of this project completed, I was not so excited about doing the second half when the other faucets arrive.

Should I consider calling the plumber and spending the hundred dollars plus when the other set of faucets arrive? I was in effect paid minimum wage for the time I spent on the first faucets. Of course, at my age that's probably all I'm worth. But, it is still difficult to hire someone to do what I can do perfectly well. "Hardheadedness" prevailed.

43

Our Last Picture Show

In the spring of 2015 with a whimper, our walk-in movie life ended in Rapid City, South Dakota. Looking to hopefully kill time one afternoon and enjoy a production of the latest Road Warrior offering, we spent a disappointing couple hours in a so-called entertainment venue trying to decide to get up and leave. Where was Mel Gibson when we needed him?

The experience started downhill early on with the volume of the sound. Having noticed in the past that movie houses turn up the decibels during the commercials and coming attractions, we tried to endure, be patient and waited for the start of the movie. The excruciating sound remained at the mind-numbing volume when the feature began.

Connie's sister left the movie and complained to someone in the lobby seemingly in charge which resulted in the sound being reduced an almost negligible amount.

For any senior citizen the movie would have been well-disciplined torture. If I had to describe it in one sentence, I would say, "Two hours of repetitive computer graphics car wrecks and fantasy with little dialogue." And we paid nine dollars each for the agony. Their expensive drinks and popcorn we declined.

Gone are the days of Fred and Ginger, Abbott and Costello, Olivia de Havilland, Kim Novak, Grace Kelly, Elizabeth Taylor, John Wayne, Gregory Peck, James Stewart, and William Holden on the big screen. Gone are movies of the caliber of *To Kill a Mockingbird, A Long, Hot Summer, Giant, Twelve Angry Men, Cool Hand Luke, The Sound of Music, Holiday Inn, Psycho,* and *Picnic.*

Prognosticators say movie theaters are slowly going to disappear. Movies, supposedly worth watching, will be seen on our home screens. It is sad to say that offerings for senior citizens will be few and very far between. With the large number of baby boomers, we could wonder if there would be more entertainment geared to our preferences. Who knows if that will happen?

Television is headed down the same path of disappointment. The number of crime dramas overwhelms the mind. The production companies feel people are obsessed with murder and mayhem. Give us a break. How many different ways can they present the good guy, bad guy ploy? It seems we are watching the same bloody programs over and over. And they wonder why young people on-the-edge go out and kill others.

Nat Geo, the History Channel, Discovery and documentaries have much greater appeal for seniors but are a minority of TV scheduling.

Thank God for the huge selection of books we seniors have at our disposal. Reading is going to receive more and more of our time.

44

Hovering Outside the Pearly Gates

The hurricane season of 2004 found us living in Lynn Haven, Florida on North Bay. We had been there five years and were familiar with the dangers and threats associated with storms. Category five Hurricane Ivan was headed our way that September and putting worried faces on us and our neighbors.

The center of landfall was expected to be west toward Fort Walton Beach and Pensacola, but major damage could be expected for a large surrounding area.

Being fully in touch with the possible damage in our area, I began preparations for weathering the storm. When we bought our house, wind shutters came with it for protection of glass from wind damage. With a large amount of glass on the bay side of our house, I knew I had to get to work.

Being told by our friends that broken windows during high winds can cause the roof to blow off the house, the wind shutters should be installed to protect against huge destruction. The "class of life" taught me again that thinking about doing a project and its execution are two very different postulates.

The wind shutters, stored in stacks under our deck, were made of aluminum and appeared to be easy to install. How many times have I been fooled by that premise? They were roughly four feet wide and perhaps eight feet long to fit the tall windows. Installation involved the ground floor and the upper floor of the house. The weight and cumbersomeness of handling the large pieces carried a huge handicap, especially on the second floor standing on a ladder.

To compound my problem, the storm had been forecast to hit late that afternoon only allowing me most of the day to get the job done. Naiveté set in as I was working on a task too large for the time allowed.

The first one-third of the shutters provided a learning experience, but soon I got the knack of putting them into place and setting the accompanying clips to secure them from blowing away. Time flitted away as I kept looking at my watch and worrying whether I could get the job done in time.

My stubborn nature dictated that I would get those shutters in place or die trying. In retrospect I should have considered other possibilities. Dying trying became a real threat.

Around ten or eleven a.m., I began to feel tired, much more tired than I should have been; more tired than I could remember. A little later I started gasping for air. Not nearly enough oxygen was getting into my lungs it seemed. I sat down for a few minutes and felt better then went back to work. Before long, I was gasping for air again and required another rest which repeated several times.

A lunch break gave me renewed energy, so I went back to work at a fierce pace. Time was dwindling. Little did I know time could be running out on me.

Continuing to have the gasping attacks followed by rest, I kept on pushing. At approximately five in the afternoon, I had finished and was dead tired. Our windows should be saved from the winds blowing foreign objects.

The howling hurricane and torrential rains made it hard to sleep, but our house survived intact with a roof over our heads.

The next morning I was out early assessing damage and learning we had lost shingles in a few places. One spot on the top front of the house had caused a leak and water stains in our great room ceiling.

The probability of hiring a roof repair guy when everyone else needed one was virtually zero. It would be a few days before I could hire someone to properly repair the leak spot. Tarring the leak area seemed my best bet knowing more rain would be falling.

The damaged area was on a highly inclined portion of the roof, so some exertion was involved to do the work and not fall. I had to get into a straining, precarious position to hang onto the bucket of tar and spatula while doing the work.

The gasping-for-air attacks started again. After finished the repair, I climbed off the roof, went into our house and lay on the floor experiencing severe tiredness, total exhaustion.

Realizing finally this gasping for air and extreme tiredness could be a message of something going on with my heart, I went to a Bay Med outpatient clinic the next morning. An EKG revealed that I had experienced a heart event. My stupidity with this was overwhelming. I flirted with a heart attack, but our Lord watched out for me.

With the help of our family doctor, I obtained a referral to a cardiologist. It took from September 2004 to early January 2005 to finally get a catheterization to learn the nature of my problem. A drug induced stress test had confirmed the need for the catheterization. The cardiologist found sixty-five percent blockage of the left anterior descending artery, the widow maker. It was not a sufficiently severe blockage for a stent. The rule of the time required seventy percent blockage for installation of a stent.

The doctor put me on a cholesterol medication, slow release nitroglycerin to take daily for keeping my heart vessels open and a medication to ensure against high blood pressure. I have never had high blood pressure but followed his orders.

The nitro and BP drug, I took faithfully for eight years until I had a reaction of low blood pressure which caused me to faint. Today I only take the cholesterol drug.

Two subsequent catheterizations over the last ten years have shown the blockage to be stable and not increasing. The doctor found other, smaller blockages which were not life threatening.

For all my friends out there who may think you are bulletproof and can handle whatever situation comes along, I will offer that is not a good choice. Be in touch with what is going on with your heart.

If an extreme shortness of breath or pain in an unusual place in your body is experienced, find a good cardiologist or an emergency room.

Everyone over fifty years should have a cardiologist to monitor the heart yearly or more often per his recommendation. Or you may be giving your family and friends a reason to come together around a tent.

45

As God Would Have It

As she and her husband were transitioning to his new job in Louisiana in the spring of 1976, she had to spend some time alone during the day at a Ramada Inn in Monroe, Louisiana, while he started his new job. Their house search had not been productive at this point, so she languished by the pool and read magazines while he was at work.

An article on skin cancer caught her attention, and she read it to learn about the malady of which she knew nothing. The article described melanoma and how to recognize the dread curse: asymmetry, contrasting shades of browns, irregular border, a size greater than a pencil eraser, and evolving size and appearance.

She learned that females have a tendency to get it on their legs while males most often find it on their backs.

Today's statistics indicate that seventy-five percent of all skin cancer deaths are related to melanoma. The good news is that the five-year-survival rate is ninety-one percent.

With this new-found information, she decided to check around her body for any signs of this highly fatal skin cancer if left untreated. She spotted a small black mole on the calf of her left leg which was slightly larger than a pencil eraser and possibly possessed the other characteristics of melanoma.

That night when she saw her husband, she showed him the article which he read in a few minutes providing the most information he had been exposed to on the subject. He asked why she chose to show him that specific article, and she showed him the innocent-looking mole on the back of her leg. They quickly agreed that a doctor should look at it.

When Dr. Kenneth Mauterer saw the spot, he immediately decided that a biopsy should be performed. After excising the mole, he sent it to a lab to be examined.

A few days later, the doctor asked her to come to his office for a consultation and informed her that the lab analysis revealed the presence of melanoma.

When he arrived after work, she and her husband hugged each other and languished over the threat which they had to confront. Praying that it had not spread was their primary concern.

Dr. Mauterer made an appointment with a surgeon in Shreveport who would remove a portion of her calf muscle for careful analysis to determine if any cells had started spreading.

She and her husband celebrated the bicentennial in a Shreveport hospital where she recovered from the surgery. An ice-cream-scoop-sized portion of flesh had been removed from her left calf. A skin graft was taken from her upper thigh to cover the wound. The doctor found no evidence of metastasizing.

Upon leaving the hospital, they were told that a chest x-ray should be taken every six months for the next five years to detect any remote possibility of melanoma. The concern was that it could spread to the lungs first in the coming years. Thankfully, the radiology exams showed no problem.

For the last forty years, Connie has spent little time in the sun. If she was outside, she applied high SP suntan lotion. No more serious skin cancer threats have been found in screenings, and she has amazingly young-looking skin.

Connie and I felt so blessed that she had read the magazine article. If she had not, she would have contracted the fatal disease. Divine intervention was at work.

God has been watching over us our entire lives. Praise to Him and His Mercy. Threats such as this cause a person to appreciate life and Our Father more than ever.

46

Robert (Pop) Trawick

In Memory of Robert (Pop) Garner Trawick

A person has the good fortune and joy of knowing maybe two or three people similar to Pop (November 8, 1934-April 25, 2015) in a lifetime. God blessed me with the privilege of being Robert's friend and gave us the opportunity to share his homemade wine, laughs, fellowship, and good times during the last fifteen years.

He would not like me sitting here with tears running down my cheeks as I struggle with this narrative, but he would understand the passion and compassion that comes with friendship. He made so many friends throughout his life with an "in-touch" approach to people. He had a way of making those around him feel important and feel that they counted in his world.

Robert started out in a hole, but through hard work and determination he dug out of it and climbed comfortably high in his eighty years. He always regretted the loss of his father at Pop's age of fifteen. Robert had to grow up quickly and hard to help his mother and he succeeded.

Being creative and entrepreneurial, he went into the business of loaning money to his buddies in the army to secure a nest egg which would place him on good financial footing when he finished his tour.

Through hard work and wise management, he was able to save their two hundred fifty acres of land and provide for his mother Nunnabelle Dozier Trawick whom he loved dearly.

Eventually becoming a dry wall contractor in the Fort Walton Beach area, he applied his talents with hard, back-breaking work and secured a good retirement for him and his wife Ginny. Robert did not have the benefits of much "book learning," but he was "business smart" and had a pleasant way with people unless they did him wrong. Then they would have a problem.

When I was fourteen or fifteen, he would occasionally show up at a dove shoot, usually at Frank Spooner's waterhole. My brother Lloyd and others would be present, but Pop stood out as the one who allowed essentially no doves to fly over him; they went in his bag. Not knowing of his skeet shooting prowess, I was amazed at his efficiency and production on the game field.

I hardly knew him since he was eleven years older and associated more with the older guys his age such as Lloyd, Larry Batchelor and others.

In the late '60s I was invited to a duck shoot at Spooner Springs with Pop shooting adjacent to me. When the mallards were flushed, I may have knocked down two or three, but Pop got them in the tens. The best use of my time was to help him pick up his ducks.

When in his thirties, Pop created quite a persona when he left Fort Walton and came visiting in Seminole County, arriving with a hot, beautiful car and a lady to match.

He once related to me of being chased by State Patrolmen for a long distance from Seminole County as he headed back to Florida. He was doing well until they blocked off a bridge and trapped him. The size of the fine he did not reveal, but it must have been hefty.

Robert, Lloyd and I shared the pleasure of a couple of trips to the Midwest for pheasants circa 2000. We went on a cage-raised-birds hunt and on another which was advertised as wild birds.

On the wild bird hunt, we were riding in a vehicle when a ringneck ran across the road, and I was the only one who saw him. When Pop and I got out of the vehicle and approached the location of the pheasant, I made an assumption that he was my bird. Unknowingly Pop did not see it that way.

As the bird cleared the ground and took air, I waited for him to fly some distance, so I did not put a full load in him and damage the meat. As I was about to squeeze the trigger, the bird exploded and fell to the ground. Robert smiled and I complained, but I was aware he could get a little self-possessed when a bird took to wing, so we laughed about it.

Pop was a communicator and enjoyed a good conversation. Once he was talking and my mind wandered. He sensed I was not listening and said, "You are not even listening to me."

Other instances of not listening in my life had been experienced, but he is the only one who recognized the inattention and called me on it—a perceptive guy. I laughed and quickly focused on what my good buddy had to say.

Pop often expressed how lucky he was to have Ginny. He said, "She is a good person and really takes care of me." Yes, he was fortunate to have such an attentive, loving life mate. Ginny, a precious and devoted lady, was exactly who Pop needed as a wife.

Samuel B Mills

On his birthday in November 2014 we had the pleasure of joining a large number of Robert's friends for a celebration organized by Junior and Atherlone Trawick. Held at what is called "The Big House," the old Brandy Trawick family home, a jam-packed crowd enjoyed food and fellowship in Robert's honor.

Atherlone had produced a video of pictures of Pop, family and friends over his lifetime which was enjoyed by everyone. It was comprehensive, lengthy and well done. My good friend shed a couple of tears displaying the humanity which was a huge part of him.

Thanks, Pop, for making a contribution and a difference in my life and others who could call you a friend. A stamped-out-one-time original, you will be missed in a large way. God bless you, and God rest your soul.

47

Prominent

A few months back in the "75 years ago" portion of the Donalsonville News, I noticed that a young lady was referred to as coming from a "prominent family." Being a student of subtlety and the sublime over the years, the statement caught my attention and provoked a review in my mind of how our residents' thinking has evolved over the years.

The word "prominent" was not only used in newspapers but applied in open discourse when referring to people. The most important common denominator for the prominent of the times was wealth; a higher level of education could possibly get a person into the "club."

We have to wonder how the decision was made of declaring someone prominent or by omission banishing them to the "other" class. Surely detailed research of financial records was not used to place the person in or out of the anointed category. Perceptions ruled: houses lived in, parties with "prominent" friends, cars driven, and expensive trips taken.

Highlighting the privileged came easy in the newspaper because with the power of the pen, the author's perceptions authorized him to declare prominence or not. No evidence had to be provided since via print readers had been trained to believe.

This negative of days gone past has disappeared. If someone were called prominent today, challengers to the title would step forward to protest and not with polite words. A person referred to as being prominent would probably want to disagree with the description as well.

The word prominent no longer divides us which is a good thing. The culture change associated is one of the byproducts of recent generations which we can praise.

48

Californy Or Bust

In May the year 2000, along came another one of my wild ideas. It seemed so tame at the moment but the "jungle" came later, in spades. Aware of the beauty of the California cost line and its rich vistas, I decided it would be an adventure for our family to take a cross country trip on a train which would track the coast with the final destination being San Francisco.

With the only choice being Amtrak, I had concerns before making the reservations, but wondered how much could they screw up a trip. Booking a private cabin with beds for Connie, Jackie age fourteen, and me, a sitting area, and a private bath, I endeavored to travel as comfortably as possible.

When the booking agent told us we would have to board the train at 4:00 a.m. in Chipley, Florida, I developed a minor flustering deep in my stomach. For such enjoyment, sacrifices had to be made and we were up to muster on the need.

Waiting on the train at this God-forsaken time in beautiful Chipley found us bright-eyed, anticipatory and slightly grouchy. At fourteen Jackie only needed the slightest excuse to get "ill" and fully lived up to her reputation.

The train was late and became later, as we stood by our pile of luggage. One hour late it chugged into town and stopped for us and only another person or two. In concert Karma, fate, bad juju and providence had started laying their trap for us. Little did we know what they had cooking, but they had spent an abundance of time planning their evil ways.

As we boarded the train, a porter helped move our luggage to our room and politely held out his hand. The room was nice and comfortable for a train ride; the bathroom small with compact sink, toilet and shower. My advice for the more rotund among us is don't take a train ride. Things won't fit, such as you.

With the scenery zipping by, we settled in to enjoy. The North Florida landscape we were so familiar with did not exactly spellbind us.

The train had to make stops along the way for a few minutes to pick up and let off passengers, and unfortunately it had to take longer holding times at points where a railroad track crossed the train's path. As we listened to the mumble among passengers, we learned that a big railroad owned all of the tracks, so the right-of-way was always theirs. Many more of these surprise stops were on the way.

About an hour or longer was lost in New Orleans with picking up passengers and yielding right-of-way. The clock kept ticking as we became six hours behind schedule then eight.

With the food and food service being fantastic, we had no complaints along those lines. Even Jackie approved of the dining room and the offerings.

As I remember, we were to spend two nights on the train and arrive in San Francisco late evening of the third night. Sleeping on a train cannot be associated with deep slumber. With the clack, clack, clack of the rails and the slight side to side swaying, packing my bags for a trip to sleepy town was a huge waste. Connie and Jackie slept like they were in mother's womb.

Chugging through the deserts of Arizona, suddenly the train came to a stop. Not yet noticing the change of temperature in the cabins, we were told that the trains cooling system had ceased working. This was June and we were in the middle of the hot Arizona desert, not the best place to lose air conditioning. People were told to stay in their seats "and suffer." Amtrak began taking on the guise of the train to Hades.

After over an hour, technicians brought the system back to life and cool air began flowing with our wild cheers. Being now about a half day behind schedule, I began to assess how badly we wanted to see the beautiful California coast line.

Old Stuff, Newer Stuff, and Stuff

Arriving in Bakersfield, California, Sam's patience had been reduced to a bare thread, or as Mama often said, "I was thread bare." We had reservations at the Fairmont in San Francisco for four nights and were in danger of missing the first night while paying for it anyway.

This old "man of action" made an executive decision. We exited the "train from glory" and headed for Hertz rent-a-car. Renting a car for a four or five hour drive to San Francisco had elements of certainty, but staying on the train was a crapshoot.

Arriving at the hotel, we settled into pagan luxury. It featured an indoor swimming pool surrounded by a restaurant with exquisite food. The rooms were extravagantly furnished and beautiful with lounging robes provided. We received what anecdotal stories and advertising had highlighted and more, a classy hotel for our enjoyment.

Since we had not been on a cable car in about twenty-five years, we enjoyed taking Jackie on her first ride. Walking up and down the San Francisco hills could kill a person and had to be avoided.

A friend Connie had modeled with years before and her husband who lived in nearby Sausalito joined us for dinner one night. She and Connie jabbered and jabbered about San Francisco and Los Angeles of the sixties. They had gone on a modeling trip on a ship to Australia, so they had a long relationship with a lot shared.

Thinking Jackie would enjoy a little trip on the bay, we took a tourist-trap journey on a boat by Alcatraz Island. We had no desire to go on the island, too depressing.

A visit to the Top of the Mark for drinks brought back memories of when we dated. The Top of the Mark is a restaurant on the nineteenth floor of the Mark Hopkins Hotel where people go to enjoy sunsets, drinks, food, and the San Francisco views.

The night before we had to leave the hotel I had to figure how to get us back to Florida. The airline had an airline booking office where I could purchase tickets. Knowing that buying a ticket for travel the next day could get expensive, I was not surprised. For the low, low price of about a thousand dollars each, we could be back in Lynn Haven, Florida the next day. Wow!

When we got back home, I was able to cash in the portion of the train trip we did not take to recover most of the three thousand dollars we spent on the plane fares. Lesson learned.

Possibly Amtrak has been improved over the last seventeen years. I don't know. If anyone gets an obsession for a train trip, check it out carefully or a surprise such as we had could be coming down the pike.

We saved the day with a car rental, but missed the Pacific Coast views which had been partial motivation to take the trip; such is life. We enjoyed San Francisco and came home safely which mattered the most.

49

Terror on Econfina Creek

Circa 2005 we were living in Lynn Haven, Florida with Connie being a Red Hat Club member. For those unfamiliar, the members get their kicks by dressing up in a bodacious red hat and purple clothing every month for a meeting at a member's house, a country club, a restaurant or at the location of some activity. Being the summer months, the member appointed to organize the meeting had chosen a canoe trip down Econfina Creek for the attending members. Unknowingly for the Mills couple, this would have been a grand time to not be an attending member.

Several of our members had been on canoe outings down the creek and assured us of loads of fun and a great day. They told us that the beautiful nature and the flowing creek would soothe our bones and revitalize.

As we all started arriving at a canoe rental outlet, we secured life preserves and rented our transportation, of sorts. Sam had arrived at the ripe young age of sixty and had never been in a canoe. I longed to rent Uncle Luke's wooden bateau which would have made me feel immensely safer.

Anyone who has spent much time paddling a canoe knows a novice doesn't simply jump in one and start semi-expert navigation. A canoe is an unpredictable beast which can give a dunking as fast as a liberal can say, "Transgender." Concern must be applied to keeping the center of gravity low in the boat, or the breast stroke will soon be useful. Paddling one looks so smooth in movies but in reality, on a first day, it is nerve wracking.

Connie and I stepped into our boat with our meager belongings: soft drinks, sunglasses, and a suspicious attitude on my part.

As we embarked, the rapid flow of the water alarmed us somewhat, but I was going to trust the judgment of the group who felt we should be having fun doing this. If the creek was relatively free of debris and sufficiently wide, we should have an easy go of it. The contradiction was on the way.

About a hundred yards down the creek, a tree, roughly eighteen inches in diameter, lay across the water obstructing our passage. I did not recall reading of this on the itinerary. We observed the couple ahead of us step out of their canoe, push it under the fallen tree, and get back in the vessel. My first thought, "Why would someone have not moved the tree?" Oh! I didn't get it! The more perilous, the better in some folks eyes.

Noticing the rapids in the creek greatly exceeded my expectations, not to mention the fallen tree debris, my temperament slowly moved up my "alarm scale."

What had we gotten into?

Ahead of us the rest of our party were the happiest of canoeists having pulled into a sandbar, tied their canoes, and began munching on snacks with wine and beer. As Connie and I tied up, I said to Sam, "Sam, water and alcohol do not mix, and they sure as hell don't mix on this fast flowing creek with debris everywhere." Sam agreed wholeheartedly. Our friends insisted that we have some of their wine, but I semi-graciously declined but Connie relented. I wanted to be sure we rode back home in our car and not a "bone wagon."

During our visit with friends, we learned a few had already turned over the canoes and possessions had been lost. One couple did not make it from the embarkation point before they took a dunk. All were affected by how funny this had been. Oh! We are having fun now!

Noticing a darkening sky and a rumbling not far away, I prayed for no thunderstorm to further complicate this harrowing trip.

We came upon a smaller fallen tree that lay slightly submerged in the water completely blocking the creek. A turnover here would be as easy as falling over a log, literally. I paddled fast and straight at the tree in hopes of passing over it at a right angle which would save us from a turn over. Luckily we made it; so far, no capsizing for Sober Sam.

Mother nature was going to have her way as clouds darkened and lightening came closer to us, too close for any kind of comfort. As it was about to flood, guess who had to go to the bathroom? My sweet love had chosen precisely the wrong moment for nature's call. Urging her to negotiate with nature, she feigned deafness.

We decided it would be easier on the bank than over the side of the unsteady canoe. Who would want to go bottom up with their pants down? This was a swampy area, so concern for hungry alligators came to mind.

As Connie made it back to the canoe, the bottom completely fell out of Saint Peter's Pond. The large downpour caused our concern that the canoe would fill up to a great extent and sink it or cause a problem navigating. We found little six-ounce drink cups and started bailing water. Asking Connie if we were having fun yet, she did not answer.

After about thirty minutes of a huge rain with lightening striking all around us, the rain gods cut us some much needed slack. I returned to my task of guiding and paddling us down the creek to the pick up point.

Considering the storm and the treacherousness of the waterway, I fully expected to see an old friend's body floating by at any time. It was that dangerous. Asking around, I determined that we could have been the only ones who did not suffer an overturned boat.

Amazed at how far down the creek we had to travel to get out of this hellhole, we finally found the pickup point around four o'clock, about five or six hours after we started.

Our tired aching bodies wanted to go home and get in a hot shower so badly. Talking with a red hat member, I suggested letting the same person plan all of the outings since she really understood how to have fun.

The following day on the internet I researched Econfina as a canoeing creek. It was rated as the only stream in Florida recommended to be used by only the highest skilled canoeists, total confirmation of the high risk trip we had taken. A number of the participants were past sixty-five and flirting with death. Connie and I had never thought of ourselves as outdoor enthusiasts. The next time we rode rapids would be in a shower in a Holiday Inn, no paddle required.

Part III Stuff

50

Life

It is probably within everyone to wonder what future life will be like when we are young teenagers. The natural tendency would be to tell ourselves things will fall into place with a minimum of challenging, unpleasant and possibly regrettable events. Being naturally idealistic, young people have no idea what life will truly offer.

But reality raises its devious head as the years go by: loved ones die, opportunities are missed, failures drop out of the sky, and the predicaments of life charge forth. As we reflect back, we learn that those things to an extent are guaranteed in everyone's life. The huge variables are their magnitude and their effect on us. We are at the mercy of fate in perilous occurrences. As far as what can be controlled, how we handle the disappointments can be the only sensible answer.

In the mid-eighties Connie and I attended a seminar entitled "Life Training." The central theme of the presentation was "life is the way it is." Those six words sound rather mundane and simplistic, but they communicated a message that lingered. Fretting extensively about what happens to us is fruitless. Rather, we should accept happenstance as life, and find a way to move on as difficult as it may be.

We venture off into the world at the mercy of fate and life. Terrible things can happen to any of us. To live a long existence without a major "earth-shaking" is blessed good fortune. When these terrible "disruptors" to life materialize, we need someone to turn to. God serves a huge purpose by being there to help and comfort us. Without Him, we are fighting a huge, desperate battle alone. With Him we have hope and the blessings of His grace.

"Wishful fairness" in life does not exist and is a waste of time; there is only life. Regardless of how unfair it seems, the same has happened to others, or worse. We can take solace by looking around at others carrying a heavier burden.

Having turned seventy-one, I can look back and say to myself, "This is what life is." In the proper perspective, life and God have been good to us. When I take into account that we live better than ninety-nine percent of the people in the world, life has been more than fair to us. We live in the greatest country and the best county on earth. Dear friends, dear relatives, and a loving church round out our lives.

Regardless of what happens to us in the future, we have been extraordinarily blessed by God. We will take our lumps and deal with whatever life brings.

51

Locked-Down

About thirty years ago I read an article which hypothesized relationships of high school classmates stay largely locked-down and fixed in stone the day they depart on their separate paths. The theory of a "relationship memory" of sorts dictates how and if personal transactions among classmates occur in the future. However a person felt about a given classmate and however the classmate felt about him or her were probably going to remain fixed to an extent in the future.

We may suspect that adulthood would break down barriers and remove most of the locks, but that is seldom the case.

Over the decades I have had the opportunity to make observations to check the theory for its accuracy. I have experienced the opportunity to interact or not with my fellow classmates both within the confines of a class reunion and in other opportunities outside such a somewhat formal and organized meeting place.

Also, I have had the benefit of going to my wife's reunions which were much larger with a class of two hundred plus. This provided an opportunity to consider class size influence. My perception was that those in larger classes remained subject to the same "rules of interaction" as the smaller ones. The same groups assembled to visit each time.

In my opinion the theory of locked-down relationships has merit. It is not nearly perfect but is a descriptive rough measure. Today that small group of people I felt so comfortable with are still those I seek out and interact with. Over the years I have added only two or three to the group.

The status quo persists with classmates with whom I had minimal relationships in high school.

During high school, teenagers find ways to form groups or cliques. The cliques occur for various reasons: participating in sports, being from the same neighborhood, going to the same church or having similar interests are things that may contribute to a bond. To a great extent the cliques define their relationships the rest of their lives, but can limit their interactions with others.

The city cliques were much larger than the country cliques because of more city students being in close proximity, going to church together, celebrating birthdays reciprocally, etc.

The tightness of cliques was exhibited in subtle ways, and an individual seldom tried to join an established clique unless he or she relocated into the area and sought out the group without knowledge of all the subtleties, or the clique sought them as a desired member.

Those outside the clique communicated very differently with members of the clique as compared to how the group members interacted with each other because of common ground and common experiences. Having commonalities that bind tend to solidify relationships and excludes outsiders.

Being a close observer of people, I have cataloged reams of data in my mind. I have learned that people communicate huge information about themselves by what they don't do. What they do is so clouded in subtleties while what they don't do is honest and open to the world. What they don't do can have a huge impact on those around them and on themselves.

What we are today is chiefly a sum total of all things which reinforced us, choices we made and chances we took. One of the subtleties in this is trust. As Stephen Covey stated so well in his book "Seven Habits of Highly Effective People," "To establish trust someone must take a risk." Human nature encourages us to avoid risk and thus the positives of the trust which can come with it.

52

Just Imagine

Imagine that you cannot respond to long sentences or questions because you cannot remember the beginning of the communication.

Imagine that you want to respond to people, but you cannot remember the words to use.

Imagine that you can remember only basic food preferences and have to ask your caregiver whether you like a given offering.

Imagine ordering a hamburger and not knowing which condiments you prefer.

Imagine the inability to bathe yourself because you cannot do a good job, because of not being able to remember what you have washed and what you haven't.

Imagine watching a TV program and having no ability to understand the plot. You can only enjoy the current scene and what happened in it.

Imagine not being able to readily share your life and learn of other's lives through communications with those you love and care for.

Imagine when you see anyone you know, you may remember their face but not their name.

Imagine that a substantial portion of your life is spent frustrated by lost things: earrings, makeup, glasses, clothes, etc.

Imagine having little appreciation for order in your life. Your brain is jumbled and your surroundings lack order resulting in frustration.

Imagine not being so caring about things which used to be a high priority in your life.

Imagine never knowing a schedule of what is planned in your life and what is happening next. When anything happens that includes you, it is virtually a surprise.

Imagine being so dependent on a caregiver that you worry about something happening to the person and want them near you all the time.

Imagine being frightened as night falls, and the shadows get longer. You want the shades closed because of some unknown fear: sundown syndrome.

Imagine not being able to take care of your personal appearance as you used to, resulting in dependence on someone to help.

Imagine a fear of unfamiliar environments. The home is a safe place, and only a few familiar places can be tolerated.

Imagine not understanding what is going on with your health. This is God's blessing and His way of protecting the person from undue anxiety.

If you live to be eighty-five you have a fifty percent chance of experiencing all of the above. The chances increase every year after age sixty.

This narrative is to promote Alzheimer's awareness. If the reader can find a way to contribute to Alzheimer's research or participate in an Alzheimer's clinical trial, do so. Most people will eventually be affected by this dreaded affliction either directly, by caring for someone, or knowing someone who suffers with the curse.

53

Time

Tick, tock goes the clock as our most precious gift disappears never to be replaced. Conservation of time is an interest in which we all can participate, or not. How should we use time best to get what we want or need? Are we focused on the right things? Do we think long term or simply live for the moment?

Good time utilization is largely prioritization. We often say or hear others speak, "I don't have time for that." The things for which we do not have time go wanting while the list of not-well-considered priorities get attention. To get the most service out of time, we should ask what are priorities and what things are relegated to the "I-don't-have-time" list. We also must learn to say, "No," when others' demands encroach unfairly on our time.

Our priorities tend to be somewhat tied to short term thinking. Speaking of not having enough time, we all had enough time to dress today. We all had time to eat and drink. These are short term priorities.

A portion of time consumption is optional: Do I go to the movie or go to the beach? We are considering our wants and what will best satisfy them.

One of the principal abuses of time revolves around people that are close to us. Usually, no one is closer than family. Family is important—or at least it should be—depending upon transgressions that may have occurred along the way among individuals or groups.

In our later years it would seem that not having regrets would be a desired goal. Old age with fewer regrets is tied to how we used our time in our younger years. Did we prioritize spending time with those we love? Did we show affection with words and actions frequently? Did we help those in need? People who can say, "Yes," to these questions have enlarged their lives. They have maximized feelings of contentment through their choices, and are more likely to be at peace. In our senior years we could still have some regrets but a lot fewer than we would have had if we had ignored people.

When we declare that we do not have time for human interactions and helping others, we have not set the right priorities. Longer term there will probably be regrets.

Life gives us a finite number of hugs, kisses, and displays of affection and caring. One day the hugger or the "huggee" will not be around. Always being aware of this, and taking time for others will promote happiness and a sense of well-being throughout our lives.

54

Symbols

Since the beginnings of civilization, people have cherished symbols. The first symbols were probably etchings on cave walls. With the coming of Jesus, the cross took on a special and sustained meaning to all Christians. Our flag is a symbol of love for our country, of the survival of our republic and for what it stands. Wedding rings are a symbol of love and commitment.

Human nature provides a special inborn need for us to have and hold symbols near and dear to our hearts. Symbols tell us who we are and can be a source of pride. People hold out pictures of their children, of whom they are so proud, as symbols. Others hang onto special gifts from those who came before us or from those they presently hold dear. Symbols of accomplishments are held closely to the heart.

In my life two symbols dominate in importance: my wedding ring and my college class ring. The wedding ring I will have worn for forty-four years on Jan 20, 2017. The class ring has been on my finger for forty-seven years. Loss of either of these would be heart-breaking, so I have held them close with great care.

The class ring has an interesting history. Having put it on proudly in 1970, I knew it was my very important symbol of accomplishment to be revered the rest of my life.

Lucky for me my finger is the same size it was when I first put it on. Many class rings have been banished to a "junk drawer" because they would not go on the digit anymore.

Only five places I allowed my class ring to be: on my finger, in my pocket, in the locked car's console, in the mail back to the supplier of the ring, or by the sink if I were taking a shower. Laying it down in a public restroom to wash my hands, I avoided one hundred percent over the years. Instead it went into my pocket during clean up time.

Always hating to take it off, I have had to replace the stone twice over the years. Doing hard work and banging it against things took a toll. Each time I insured it and prayed for the best in its absence.

On those occasions when I had surgery, the ring stayed in the console in our car. No way would I trust hospital personnel with something I regarded as so valuable.

Why have I treated this seventy-five dollar ring (1970 price) as such a treasure? It represents accomplishment. Graduating from college made Loziane and Sam proud, me too. Mama was not there except in spirit, but I know she had a huge smile on her face. The degree that came with it opened doors and helped this old plodder rise up and throw off the shackles of poverty. It provided a comfortable life which would never have been possible otherwise. Connie and I have lived the American dream.

As for my other symbol, my wedding ring, the only reason I have taken it off is for surgery. It stayed in the console with my class ring during medical procedures that required no jewelry. Being much smaller than the class ring, I did not have to take it off when bathing since minimal dirt and germs trapped under it was not a problem.

The wedding ring is a symbol of the "forever bond" I share with the one person on earth I love the most. It will always be with me, as will she, until death do we part.

Thanks to God for His nudges in the right direction so many years ago. He provided Connie as a life mate, and He gave me the desire, the intelligence, and the perseverance to get a college degree.

55

The Pretentious Among Us

Having passed the seventy-first year of my life, I often reflect on the lessons learned and the pitfalls one should try to avoid. Awareness of pitfalls helps but does not always guarantee an individual will stay clear of them every time one appears.

One of the things I genuinely love about Seminole County is the shortage of pretentious people. When one is found, the person should be put in a cage on display for everyone to observe. To do that, one may have to be kidnapped in an adjoining county and brought here. Pretentiousness can be easier to notice when the "affected" person gets right up next to you within hugging distance.

Connie and I once lived in a community with precisely five pretentious people, two of the five were married to each other. These people were outrageously amazing and entertaining to observe. Things they all had in common: a position up the financial scale, bubbly personalities, and a desire for control over those around them. In the neighborhood they were regarded as "power brokers" who kept the community "in line" so subtly.

When I encountered one of them at a party, I could predict his/her behavior in advance consistently. First came the award winning smile and hello as if I had escaped from a desert island after twenty years. Next came the hug and perhaps the air kiss on the side of my head. And lastly a thirty-second to one minute conversation that evoked caring. It did not communicate caring, only evoked it. Then off to the next person with an approximation of the same robot act I witnessed. At the next party I "enjoyed" a full replay of what happened at the last one.

As the evening wore on, the pretentious gravitated to those who were "under their spell," the close friends with whom they had some level of honesty.

It is remarkably easy to separate the pretentious from the genuine. The pretentious depend totally on "syrupy words of charm" to maintain their hold on the person. The "real people" use genuine caring words and caring actions. It is the actions that best convey one's positions and feelings: longer, interesting conversations which relate an interest in your life, walking across a room to sit with you, the "real" in the demeanor, and a lack of the bubbly words of power control.

Obviously, we fit in this neighborhood about as well as a burger flipper at a neurologist convention. The pretentious sensed that I "cut them no quarter," so those thirty-second conversations would never get any longer. As Popeye said, "I yam who I yam."

It is so wonderful to be back home among real people who are what they are. What you see is what you get. We can so easily be ourselves without enduring the actions and games of manipulation.

56

From For-Granted to Precious

In youth, children generally take things for granted. They take what may be called basics for granted: food, clothes, shelter, loved ones, etc. Youth much better understand and recognize the presence of things, not so much the absence. Therefore basics and people have less value during the formative years as compared to later life.

Life becomes a long process from taking-for-granted to grasping the importance and preciousness of those things that bring comfort and joy. Close loved ones stand separately from the other items. Through growing into adulthood and hard work, individuals can continue their supply of food, clothes, and shelter. If they are lucky and committed to enjoying a good adult life, an uninterrupted flow of the basics of life can be had.

Barring a streak of hard luck, the fundamentals of life can be taken for granted to an extent. Things appreciate in value generally because of uniqueness, scarcity and the threat of loss.

In youth a child may experience the loss of a loved one, but it takes on a different meaning versus the same loss in adulthood unless it is a parent or sibling. The loss of those close can rock a life, but in youth it takes on less gravity than when older. The length and quality of a relationship have a major bearing on its importance to the participants.

The number of years that we spend with a loved one is directly proportional to their importance and preciousness. Therefore as we get older, the length of relationships usually defines the measure of the eventual loss.

The passing of a son or daughter in middle age can have a devastating effect on a parent. Having seen the pain on Daddy's face when losing a forty-year-old son, I can personally attest to this. He did not take the son for granted. Rather he understood how precious he was and gained joy and comfort from his presence.

Experiencing painful losses of mates after long, successful, happy marriages can be the most painful. First we may witness the loss of some of our friends' spouses and see first-hand how hurtful it can be. Fear of deprivation can set in as we know that can be us at some point.

As we get into the long-shadows portion of our lives, thankfulness for every day and for ours and our spouse's health come to the fore. The lucky among us come to grips with how precious that special person is. We well comprehend that there is only one heartbeat between us and devastating pain and loss.

Thankfulness must be a defense mechanism inside us that activates as we get closer to witnessing the deprivation of a spouse and the earth-shattering loss accompanied. Some of us are canny enough to communicate to our loved ones their importance and value in order to soften the blow of the inevitable and to ensure words are not left unsaid.

For-granted and preciousness are both players in our lives. Of the two, the latter is the most rewarding part of our existence because it is what helps confirm us as human. To understand the value of others and appreciate the love they bring are among God's greatest gifts. The experience tends to maximize as we reach our senior years— by His design.

57

It Went Where?

Could someone slow down this carnival ride? I keep trying to drag my foot off the float to slow it, to break the pace but to no avail. It speeds up relentlessly. It is paradoxical. The more I drag my foot, the faster it speeds.

When I was eighteen, the years passed like a Model A chugging up a hill. The things that I looked forward to and wanted to happen "now" seemed to have a hard time arriving, so time seemed unfriendly, almost an enemy. Well, a sincere hello to my new friend.

In my younger years I kept looking for a faster life until I found myself behind the wheel of a Ferrari which could breakneck speed me down the road of life. As the years flittered by, it slowly became way too fast for my liking. Who wants to see the trees of life as a green blur? Stopping at the mailbox has become a challenge—going too fast.

This same time last year seems as if it were almost yesterday. Everything in between is a fast fog. Where did all the time go? With my "year older" appearing to be only a couple months, somebody got cheated.

We feel a need to be busy to get those things done which go lacking, but the busier we get, the faster the minutes zip by. Maybe I will spend more time studying my "do list." Surely that will bring things to a crawl.

As I have reached a ripe old, pruned-up age, I witness friends and relatives around me moving into the last sunset. How close is my last day and last moment? What should I be doing knowing the one last surprise could pop any day?

Samuel B Mills

After much consternation, it seems the best salvation is to thank the Lord for the nanoseconds I have and be glad they are mine to use. The moments go quickly, but that makes them much more precious. Things in short supply are always highly valued. Treasuring the time with the ones I love goes to the top of the bucket list; in fact, it *is* my bucket list.

58

What Rattles the Brain

Culture can be defined as the way people "think, talk, work and act." As we get older, we see the evolution of our culture in both good and bad aspects. One could make a strong case that in the last forty years our way of life has degraded to an extent. In the last eight years, it appears to have accelerated toward the dark side.

An interesting observation regarding our culture is how the media responds when "someone of note" passes away. Back in the '50s and '60s a famous person's death grabbed five minutes or less on the network nightly news. It had happened. People were informed. Praises were offered. Solemn words were spoken, and the world went on about its business.

Contrast that with what happens today when a celebrity, not just a Hollywood celebrity, passes. The radio and TV media will not hesitate to interrupt a scheduled program to do a breaking news piece. Dependent on the media's perceived importance of the individual, the break could be short or totally dislodge the programming of the moment. Often the news chooses to immerse us into reels and reels of accomplishments, praise, interviews of those who new the person, etc. A "special," an hour or longer in length, may be devoted to analyzing and "hallelujahing" the individual's life. If aliens landed from another planet in the midst of this, they could easily suspect the person was a "deity" or someone much higher than the populace in general.

The individual who left the stage is actually only one of us. He or she was blessed with special talents or gifts from God and used them.

Sometimes the gifts are used well and sometimes not. They get up in the morning, put their pants on like us, eat like us, use the bathroom like us, and so forth—just one of us.

The media steps in and talks and acts so craftily we are apt to believe this person was someone much better than we are. They elevate this person almost to a mini-god in certain cases. They do the most outrageous job of this when actors pass, expounding seemingly to no end. "He or she made these wonderful movies, earned a huge pile of money, and greatly influenced our lives." Being so much more special than "average Joe," we "plebeians" should openly mourn their passing and miss them forever.

A few years ago Robin Williams ended his life via suicide. We should give him credit. He was a comic genius. He entertained us with a number of movies. He was fantastic as Mork in the TV series "Mork and Mindy." But he led a flawed life no differently from the rest of us. In the bulk of his career, he was in and out of psychological care. He abused alcohol and drugs and allowed a fortune to slip through his hands; he was one of us but different mainly in magnitude.

Our media and culture communicated, "Now that he is gone, we should overdose on his life for a while." The days of five minutes on the TV network news are gone. The media loves celebrity deaths. It sells print advertisements, publications, ads and more. Turning a person into a "saint" can be profitable.

Celebrities have tremendous and sometimes unwanted influence on our lives. Liberal Hollywood throws its money around to causes which basically try to control our lives. They nonchalantly attend fund raising political dinners that cost $50,000 per plate. Being so affluent, they are completely out of touch with the middle class and its struggles. The many control mechanisms they support: higher taxes, federal control of education, gun control, welfare, and so forth have little effect on them.

Our misguided culture says we should praise the celebrities profusely, but a soldier who loses his life on some mountain in Afghanistan thousands of miles from his loved ones is relegated to a four inch obituary in the hometown newspaper and a flag-draped coffin. He chose to risk his life for our country. A significant recognition of his life sounds appropriately compelling. How does that compare to a celebrity who gave his life to enjoying himself?

59

Alzheimer's

The purpose of this narrative is to pass on information that I wish so much I could have possessed nine years ago.

Alzheimer's disease is one of the cruelest diseases contracted by human beings. If the person is strong and survives to the very late stages, it robs him or her of all faculties: the ability to remember, the ability to move, control of bowels and bladder, eyesight, hearing, sense of smell, and eventually the ability to swallow which results in death. An Alzheimer's patient's independence disappears as a result of the loss of capabilities. Complications throughout the later stages take most lives.

The earlier Alzheimer's disease can be detected the better. A couple of drugs, Aricept and Namenda which mask the symptoms can help the person to be functional longer.

Evaluation by a capable neurologist is the best means of receiving a diagnosis though not all neurologists have been trained in the procedures. The diagnosis will give a ninety percent probability of the presence of Alzheimer's if the disease is thought to be present. Today the only known means of getting a one hundred percent accurate diagnosis is to study the brain during autopsy. Both the Mayo Clinic in Jacksonville and Shands Clinic at the University of Florida do a good job of diagnosis.

No known cure exists, but the amount of research being conducted is substantial. Clinical trials are being sponsored by private laboratories, major drug companies, and universities all over the world. The disease is so complicated that the testing of various races and ethnicities is important to detect any variations in response to the test drugs.

Early detection has not been mastered since the disease comes on over a period of fifteen to twenty years or longer. Diagnosis in first stages with today's medical capabilities is impossible because the changes in the person and the brain are so slow and subtle early on. Progress is being made with possible blood, brain, or other tests to identify Alzheimer's far upstream to the appearance of symptoms.

People who inherit the APOe4 gene have an increased risk of getting Alzheimer's. It does not mean they are going to get it nor does it mean people without the gene have no risk of getting Alzheimer's. DNA testing is available for those who wish to learn the presence or absence of the gene.

Signs to watch for in yourself or loved ones are listed below:

1. Forgetting how to drive to or from a familiar place
2. An avid reader having to go back and reread a previous part of the book in order to follow the plot
3. Often asking to have things repeated when a person has good hearing (Focus is affected by AD. The first time a message is heard it is garbled. The second time, with focus achieved, the information may be received.)
4. Unexplained fender benders or accidents (Spatial relations are affected. Alzheimer's patients do not see what a normal person does. They may misjudge distances and sizes of things. Depth perception is altered.)
5. Frequent loss of items (Everyone can misplace keys occasionally but an Alzheimer's patient can spend a significant portion of their time looking for items: lipsticks, clothes, kitchen utensils or dishes, wallet or pocketbook, etc. In slight exaggeration everything can be lost part of the time.)
6. Asking someone to repeat something said only a few minutes before (The short term memory is most affected. The person may well remember what happened in childhood but not what happened a minute ago.)
7. Anxiety and depression (Depression is not something the person is always aware of. There is latent, or hidden depression that a

seemingly happy person experiences. Anxiety comes with depression and usually easily detected. Fidgeting with the fingers, constantly moving around, feelings that something is going to happen that the person cannot control, loss of cognition, licking the lips, etc. Medication can temporarily stop anxiety though in some cases it may be the harder symptom to control.)
8. Loss of knowledge of the environment (At a point an Alzheimer's patient may forget where things are kept or where to store them. Kitchens will have things mixed in the cabinets or put in strange places.)
9. Things are left where they lie when a project is finished. (Outside gardening implements are left on the ground where the project is completed. Things are pulled out of a drawer in the house, used and left where they were being used. In general, things are not returned to their storage places.)
10. Lack of organization (The ability to organize anything is gone. Makeup cases get jumbled and cluttered. Closets have no rhyme nor reason for where clothes are hung. Things may pile up around a person's favorite chair where neatness prevailed before. A car can become piled with clutter as compared to previously.)
11. Confusion (The limited ability to capture and recover information can cause confusion. A conversation about possibly traveling somewhere can be had, and the next day the person is seen packing a suitcase. When going to the doctor with a spouse, confusion about who the doctor's appointment is for may arise. Bits and pieces of information are recovered from memory resulting in confusion.)
12. Words don't flow as they did previously. (When talking, the person might forget words causing stopping and starting or incomplete sentences.)
13. One does not know things like the day of the week, the month/date, the year or in what state, city or county one resides.
14. Not participating actively in group conversations (Focus has deteriorated to the point that a group conversation becomes

confusing. The person can't follow the conversation and stops or greatly reduces participation. There is also the fear of being socially embarrassed by asking the same question repeatedly. One-on-one conversation goes much better.)
15. Inability to learn new tasks (If a person with early stage Alzheimer's tries to learn to use a computer, he is doomed to frustration. Part or all of whatever is learned in one session is gone by the next attempt. Operating a new home appliance may be difficult or impossible.)

Ten percent of those aged sixty-five and older are estimated to have Alzheimer's. The number rises to forty-seven percent for those older than eighty-five. Every five years after age sixty-five, a person's probability of getting the disease doubles. With the large baby boomer population, medical and long term care facilities are going to be challenged to handle the increasing number of cases. Today an estimated 5,400,000 in our country have Alzheimer's—which number will get much larger.

Presently all is not lost when a person is diagnosed, the most important step. An Alzheimer's patient should acquire the medications known to reduce the symptoms. Symptom reduction will become less and less as the disease progresses, but the drugs help the individual to be functional longer.

If a person has the resources, he can participate in a clinical trial. The clinics which administer studies are in great need of volunteers. There is a website, clinicaltrials.gov, a fairly well maintained listing of all the trials in progress with contact information. Most drug companies will pay mileage and motel expenses for participants. It takes perseverance to get into the trials, but it is readily doable. Don't count on your family doctor to help with joining a clinical study. He/she does not have the time nor staff to find clinical trials for patients.

A major breakthrough in research is expected within the next five to ten years. The drug company that comes out first with medicine that prevents, arrests, or reverses the disease will receive the pot at the end of the rainbow.

A study under way in Columbia, South America is testing the preventive properties of a Genentech sponsored drug, Crenezumab, chosen to be used among twenty-five competing medicines. An extended family in the country gets the disease as early as age thirty-five.

Having become informed by necessity and hard knocks, I truly hope everyone finds this helpful in understanding a major threat to senior citizens and those who love and care for them. If anyone has questions, I can be contacted on my Facebook website, Sam's Place.

Made in the USA
Lexington, KY
07 December 2019

58275810R00120